Mr Francis X Kuhn

Member since 1960
Life Member since 1978

another
door
opens

Jeffrey A. Wands

another door opens

*A Psychic Explains How
Those in the World of Spirit
Continue to Impact our Lives*

ATRIA BOOKS

New York   London   Toronto   Sydney

ATRIA BOOKS

1230 Avenue of the Americas
New York, NY 10020

Copyright © Jeffrey A. Wands

All rights reserved, including the right to reproduce this book or portions thereof
in any form whatsoever. For information address Atria Books, 1230 Avenue of the
Americas, New York, NY 10020

ISBN-13: 978-0-7432-7964-2

ISBN-10:   0-7432-7964-6

First Atria Books hardcover edition September 2006

10 9 8 7 6 5 4 3 2 1

ATRIA BOOKS is a trademark of Simon & Schuster, Inc.

Manufactured in the United States of America

For information regarding special discounts for bulk purchases, please contact
Simon & Schuster Special Sales at 1-800-456-6798 or
business@simonandschuster.com.

As always, my deepest and most heartfelt thanks to my wife, Dawn, and our boys, Christopher and Robert, as well as the loving memory of our dog, Cleo, all of whom have inspired me to do better and taught me the true meaning of love and life.

Acknowledgments

My thanks to all the clients who have helped me to learn what I know about the purpose of life on earth and the higher plane, particularly to those who so generously agreed to be interviewed in order to make this book more meaningful, and to their loved ones on the other side. Martha Copeland was not actually a client, but she and her daughter Cat have helped not only me but thousands of others to gain a deeper understanding of the loving relationship that continues after death.

I am deeply grateful to Dr. Raymond Moody, Dr. Brian Weiss, Dr. Holly Shaw, Dr. Deborah Wolf, Dr. Jane Greer, and Sandy Rafman for providing the therapeutic and medical points of view.

Thank you to everyone at WALK FM radio, my listeners, and all those who have called in to my program over the years. You, too, have helped me to learn and to help others.

My gratitude to my patient and always proactive agents, Liv and Willy Blumer; to Judy Kern, who helped with every step of the writing of this book; to my editors, Brenda Copeland, who was there at the beginning, and Wendy Walker, whose insightful suggestions made it even better at the end; and to all the wonderful and supportive people at Atria, especially Carolyn Reidy and Judith Curr.

To the great staff of *The Maury Show* for giving me the opportunity to help those in need.

To my assistant, Theresa O'Kelly-Moriarty, for showing grace under pressure and always going that extra mile even when she really didn't have to.

To my friend Sergio Nicolich for having my best interest at heart and watching my back.

Each one of you, and many others whom I cannot name, has made a special and much appreciated contribution to my work and particularly to this book.

Contents

A Note to My Readers

Because I understand that those of you who are new to the idea of continuing life after death and after-death communication may find some of the concepts in this book confusing or difficult to accept, I would like to explain why I sometimes say I "know" or "believe" something that might leave you wondering, "How could he know that?" or "Why does he believe that?"

In virtually all such instances, it is what I've experienced as a psychic working with clients and communicating with those in spirit that has led me to my knowledge and beliefs. Although my work may seem unusual to you, I am really not very different from anyone who has practiced a craft or a profession over a long period of time. The more you work at something, the more information you gather about your particular field, and the more expertise you have, the better you know "how things work," so to speak. Therefore, I may, for example, say I "know" that there are no coincidences in life, or I "believe" it is fear that holds people back from finding fulfillment. When I say these things, it is because those in spirit have communicated the information to me and/or because, over the years, my clients have confirmed their validity through the outcomes they've achieved as a result of our working together.

In addition, I have found that many people are surprised to learn that I use a variety of methods derived from many different religious or spiritual traditions to help me with my work. Like those who practice Buddhism, I believe in reincarnation as a way for the soul to evolve and find its purpose in life. Yet I also use Catholic beliefs, prayer, and practices to attract positive energy and connect with my higher self. Because, to me, water signifies purity and is the source of life, I sprinkle holy water in places where lingering negative spiritual energy is causing problems for the current occupants. I even use some of the principles of feng shui, which derives from a Chinese tradition, to shift the energy in particular locations. In fact, I will use whatever ritual I can in order to bring up and connect with a higher spiritual vibration.

Those of you who have been brought up to follow a particular religion or spiritual tradition may find this eclectic approach disconcerting. I, however, was born into this kind of eclecticism. My birth father was Jewish, and my mother, born Anglican, converted to Judaism. I was never told there was a right or wrong way to connect with God or the higher power, and as I was growing up I was drawn more and more to Catholicism, whose rituals and prayers I find grounding and comforting.

That said, however, I believe there are many different ways to connect with the world of spirit, and I don't believe there is any right or wrong road to achieving spirituality. Your belief system, whether or not you label it religion, is always very personal. To me, the only thing that really matters is using your own core beliefs to make the spiritual connection in whatever way works for you as an individual. I've explored many different paths and taken from each of them whatever has been helpful to me. I don't believe there's anything wrong with combining what you get from a variety of beliefs.

So, as you read on, I invite you to keep an open mind. Don't think that my way is the right way or the only way, but do seek the way that will help you to enrich your own life by making that spiritual connection. And, finally, if it works for you, don't worry about what other people think.

Introduction: Another Door Opens

Another door opens—what exactly does that mean? Because I'm a psychic, the meaning of those words is probably a little different for me than it is for you. I've read many definitions of what it means to be a psychic, but the one that comes closest to how I feel about what I do is that a psychic is someone who is sensitive to energy, the forces beyond the physical world.

Everything that lives or has lived is composed of energy, and I feel that energy in many different ways—it can come in a dream, a sign, a feeling, a premonition, a smell, or a mental image. I compare it to being a kind of human cell phone tower, a receptor who is constantly picking up all these different forms of energy. While all of us are sent these signs and signals, most people are not sensitive to or aware of them. A typical example of this is the woman who "just happened" to get an appointment with me on her dead husband's birthday. What seemed to her nothing more than a happy coincidence I immediately recognized as her husband's way of letting her know that he was still around and involved with her life. So, although I know that everyone has the ability to tap into this soul energy and communicate with the spirit world, my access to it comes a lot more easily than it does to most people.

Therefore, from my perspective, "another door opens" means first of all that there is more than one avenue of communication available to us. We can communicate in the usual ways with other people, but we can also communicate information on a psychic or soul level. Beyond that, however, the words "another door opens" mean that when someone dies, one door may close on our ability to communicate with that person but, at the same time, another door opens to a different kind of communication.

There are an infinite number of vortexes, or doors, on this plane where souls can come through. A vortex is a point of irresistible attraction, so once we realize that all souls are pure energy, we can visualize these entry points as pulling their energy toward us. Sometimes, however, it takes a soul time to find those points and learn how to come through.

When a person crosses over, he or she experiences a degree of shock. When I do a reading for someone whose loved one has died, I'm sensitive to what the person in spirit is feeling, and what I've learned from these communications is that crossing over will be a greater or lesser shock, depending in large part on how the person died. Those who've been ill and have had some time to come to peace with the transition feel less of a jolt than those who die suddenly and may, therefore, take more time to accept their new state of being. But whatever shock is involved in the transition from one state of consciousness to another, the soul must also learn how to communicate with the living and make its continued presence felt in an entirely new way. And we, for our part, can help our loved ones to do that by making peace with their death and by prayerfully inviting them to "stay in touch."

———

But the words "another door opens" have yet another meaning. Very often the passing of a loved one opens up a new door in the life of someone left behind by changing his or her life in a profound and significant way.

The door to the spirit world opens both ways.

To me it's perfectly clear that there are many doors of communication between people in this life and also that the door between this life and the next is never locked. Those who have passed on still communicate with those they leave behind. For many people, however, that concept is extremely difficult, if not impossible to accept. I've had experiences where people in group readings (usually when someone hasn't received the message he or she wanted) have accused me of planting people in the audience. I've also been accused of "rigging" the calls I accept during my radio program.

We live in "prove-it-to-me" times, but I don't believe that psychic communication is something that can be proved—at least not right now, not with the methods we currently have available to us—because we simply can't control what comes to us and, therefore, we can't prove it in a clinical, scientific way. And, in any case, I don't consider it my job to convince anyone who doesn't want to be convinced.

Many people, however, have tried. As far back as 1882, a

group of serious scientists founded the British Society for Psychical Research; their goal was to determine whether or not scientific principles could be applied to proving or disproving the existence of a world beyond the physical. Two years later, William James, the eminent psychologist and one of the most influential thinkers of his time, became one of the founders of the American branch of the society. In the end, however, neither the British nor the American investigators were able to claim that the results of their many experiments could carry the weight of actual scientific proof.

About one hundred years later, armed with a century of advancements in science and technology, Dr. Gary Schwartz, a professor of psychology, medicine, neurology, psychiatry, and surgery at the University of Arizona, put together a research team to conduct a series of scientific, laboratory-controlled experiments with five well-known, well-respected mediums into the possibility of afterlife communication. He chronicles these progressively more stringent experiments in his book *The Afterlife Experiments* and, in the end, concludes:

> When people ask us [him and his researchers], "Are you advocating survival of consciousness," we say, "no—what we are advocating is survival of consciousness *research*." . . .
>
> The confirmation, if valid, would be earth-shaking—equal to proving the earth round rather than flat. It would be one of the most profound revelations of science in human history.

If you're skeptical, just having the experience
can open your mind and open new
doors in your life.

With or without scientific proof, however, what I do know is that there have been innumerable times when even the most stubborn nonbeliever was convinced by the validity of the messages I've delivered. One of my favorite instances of this occurred when a totally nonbelieving teamster, six feet tall with really big shoulders and a real prove-it-to-me kind of demeanor, was dragged to a reading by his wife. I could see by his body language when he sat down that he really wasn't having any of it, but his mother, whose name was Margaret, came through and gave me such specific information about nicknames, dates, anniversaries, the tattoo on his right shoulder blade, and a description of her brother, Jack, who used to get drunk all the time and give my client money, that by the time he got up to leave, he had totally changed his mind and turned into a gentle giant. Not only did he thank me profusely, but he also told me to give him a call in case I ever needed any cement. Who knows, some day I might be building a patio and take him up on that offer!

It's both interesting and significant, I think, that men of science have always been among those who are most open to the possibility of making contact with the world of spirit. Of course, one of the fundamental laws of physics is the law of conservation of energy, which states that although energy can be changed in form, it can neither be created nor destroyed. To me that means that life energy, the energy of the soul, must certainly be eternal. And if that is so, is it such a great leap to accept the fact that the energy of souls on earth and those who have crossed over can communicate with each other? In fact, the great inventor Thomas Edison was reported to have been working on a machine that would allow us to communicate with the dead. "I don't claim that our personalities pass onto another existence," he told *Scientific American*. "I don't claim anything, because I don't know anything . . . But I do claim that it is possible to construct an apparatus which will be so delicate that if there are personalities in another existence who wish to get in touch with us . . . this apparatus will at least give them a better opportunity." Unfortunately, the invention, whatever it might have been, was apparently never completed and no prototype or "work in progress" was ever found after Edison's death.

It seems inevitable that there are always going to be people who just don't want to open their minds to the possibility of life after death. They may be too caught up in the biases of their own upbringing or their own anger at someone's having been "taken" from them to see anything beyond the black and white of their own reality. Or they may simply be afraid. Fear plays a big role, not only in our willingness—or unwillingness—to accept the unknown but also in our ability to find fulfillment in our own lives. I'll be talking a lot more about fear in the pages to follow, but in my experience communicating with both the living and the dead, I have found that it's easier and more comfortable for a lot of people to believe that when we die we simply cease to exist altogether than it is to be open to the possibility that our energy lives on in a different form.

Personally, I find that attitude a little hard to understand because I'd think that people would be happy to know not only that their loved ones are still a part of their lives but also that they, too, will be part of their own loved ones' lives after they pass on. And talking about loved ones, that really is the key here, because it is the bond of love that keeps us connected even after death.

Connection, however, doesn't mean that your mother or your paternal grandfather is "up there" watching every move you make. As I'll be discussing in later chapters, there are some disturbed souls who may not yet understand that they've died, or who don't want to let the living get on with their lives, who do interfere with our daily activities. But my experience has taught me that, because the majority of our loved ones continue to love us and want the best for us even after they've crossed over, they don't want to be intrusive, and, therefore, they connect only at those times when they know it's truly important to us. I like to see it as opening and popping through a door in our lives and then popping back out and closing the door after them. But that doesn't mean they can just pop in on anyone, like a stranger barging into someone's house uninvited. I still have to laugh at the email I received from a young boy asking me if, after he died, he'd be able to watch Pamela Anderson taking a shower. While I certainly understand that for a teenage boy this possibility might bring a whole new meaning to the term "died and went to heaven," unfortunately I had to disabuse him of the notion that death would suddenly turn him into an omniscient voyeur.

———————

Beyond opening a new line of communication, however, the passing of a loved one can also open new doors for us in this life.

Just the encounter with death itself can get us to reassessing what we're doing with our own life. Maybe we've been slogging along, just putting one foot in front of the other and doing the same thing every day without giving it much thought. And then, suddenly, someone we love is gone from our life (or so it seems). That can be a really loud wake-up call. Especially when the death is what we think of as premature—the result of an accident or violence or an unexpected illness—we begin to think, if it happened to that person, it could also happen to me. If I were to die right now, how would I feel about what I've done with my life? Maybe we just decide to be kinder to ourselves, to cut ourselves some slack, or to do something we've always wanted to do but didn't think we could or should. And sometimes the entire focus and purpose of our path will change in profound and life-altering ways.

The death of a loved one can be the key to opening new doors in your life.

I'll never forget the firefighter's wife who came to see me after her husband was killed in the line of duty. The messages I gave her that day affected her so deeply that she became determined to make changes not only in her own life but also in the lives of others. As a result, she entered the public arena, became involved in politics, and wound up running for and being elected to public office.

A second example of this kind of life-altering death is the case of Carolyn McCarthy, whose husband was killed in the

Long Island Railroad massacre in 1993. At that point, she had been leading a quiet, private life, working as a nurse for thirty years, but following her husband's death, she ran for Congress on a platform advocating against gun violence and has been in office ever since.

I've never met either Ms. McCarthy or her husband, but because of what I've learned through my communications with the spirit world, I believe that her life-altering experience was not any more of a coincidence than that of the firefighter's widow. There is a higher power—whether or not you believe in it and whatever you may feel comfortable calling it—that guides all our lives. We are brought into relationships for a reason, and in both of these instances, these women were intended to meet and marry these men. And their husbands' deaths were a part of their own souls' purposes just as much and as surely as the doors they opened for the wives they left behind.

As you'll be learning, if you haven't figured it out already, people come into our lives for a reason, and there's also a reason why and when they leave us. I'm sure you, too, know someone who came into his or her own after the death of a loved one and blossomed in some unexpected way. But however unexpected or surprising the turn this person's life took, I promise you that it was meant to happen, and that the death of the person who passed on was meant to facilitate or effect that change in some way.

It may be disturbing to think that someone dies in order to change the life of a loved one left behind, but it's important to remember that the death itself is as much a part of that person's path as the change it brings about for the living. For each of them another door has opened.

I

Why Me?
The Gift That Goes on Giving

Usually when someone asks, "Why me?" it means one of two things. It's either, "Woe is me. Why did this happen to me?" or, "Wow, how did I get so lucky?" In my case it's been a little of both.

You Can Run, but You Can't Hide

I know now that I've been given a gift, but for a long time I was unable to see it as a gift. In fact, it sometimes seemed to me like a little bit of a curse. I like to think of myself as an ordinary guy, and I wanted other people to see me as normal, so for a long time I tried to hide—and hide from—my gift. I tried to fight against or just ignore my psychic abilities. But, as I've discovered, we can't always control the gifts we've been given. I couldn't just wrap up my gift and take it back somewhere to exchange it for one I thought I'd like better. And I couldn't control the messages that kept coming at me, whether I wanted them or not.

In my book *The Psychic in You,* I talked about messages I started getting and contacts I made with souls on the other side when I was a little kid. And, as I said, very often what came at me got me in trouble. I didn't know where these "insights" or apparitions were coming from, and very often I just blurted out whatever popped into my head. I remember very well the day I made my sixth-grade teacher cry when I told her that her mother was standing in the room behind her wanting to know why she was so angry with her, and then I named the song her mother had sung to her when she was a child. I certainly hadn't wanted to make my teacher sad, but her response was just one of the many unforeseen reactions to things I told people that eventually led me to want to hide my light under a bushel, so to speak.

For a long time I was afraid—and not without reason—that people would think I was weird and I'd be rejected. Then, when I grew up, got married, and had children, I was afraid of the teasing and ridicule I thought my kids would be subjected to because of the work I do. As it's turned out, my kids haven't had a problem with it (in fact they have fun with it), and neither have their friends, but I didn't know that then.

ACCEPTING MY GIFT

It may have taken me a while to figure it out—in fact, it took me well into my thirties—but I now know that I don't have to be afraid of affecting other people's lives because it is precisely the fact that I *can* impact the lives of others for the better that makes my gift so valuable. When I finally accepted how much and how many people I could help, I was able to give up my need to be normal. "Normal" for me became helping people, and when I thought of it in those terms, I actually liked what I was able to do. I always try to act from a place of doing the right thing, and I do believe that most of the time I'm making a difference. The way I've finally come to see it is this: If I were a gifted concert pianist and I never played the piano, I'd be throwing away and dishonoring my gift. I never want to dishonor my gift. Instead, I now look upon it as a call to duty from the higher power.

In truth, it seems to me that the whole concept of "psychicness" has become far more acceptable, even mainstream, in recent years. When I began my work I couldn't have imagined that programs like *Medium* and *Psychic Detectives* would ever be drawing huge television audiences or that books and personal appearances by psychics would be selling in record numbers and drawing huge crowds. All of this has come as a pleasant surprise, and I like to think that my own work has contributed in some small way to that acceptance. When I think about why it's happened, I believe there are two reasons. One is that science has been able to accomplish so much that no one imagined possible fifty years ago, and that people are more willing to accept the "possibility" of many things they formerly considered impossible. And the second reason is that, in recent years, there have been so many large-scale catastrophes, both natural and man-made, that people are eager to find some meaning in life that goes beyond their short time on earth. When life as we know it seems so fragile, it seems natural to seek some larger significance for our being here at all.

Getting back to "Why me?" however, beyond not wanting to seem weird, I was also extremely uncomfortable with the power people seemed to want to give me. Until I started getting their feedback, I didn't really understand how much of an effect I was having on people. But when I began to get calls and mail saying, "You changed my life," instead of being pleased or proud, I was very upset. I didn't want that kind of power. In fact, I hated it.

For a long time, all those fears and that discomfort held me back from accepting what I was really supposed to be doing. Instead, I tried several different businesses. At one point I even opened a restaurant. But every time I tried to get away from my gift, whatever venture I tried turned out to be a disaster—and I also wasn't happy or fulfilled.

If you keep running away from your gift,
you're really just cheating yourself.

Still, I worried about "going public," and it wasn't really until I appeared on *The Maury Show* for the first time in December 2001 that I knew I'd made peace with the path I was meant to follow. There I was, giving readings not only in front of a full studio audience but in front of millions of television viewers as well. I figured that was about as public as it gets. It was sort of like my coming-out party. But the experience also made me realize that through my work I was able to help more people than I could ever have done in any other profession I might have chosen, including the law, which had been one of my early career choices. Maybe in other circumstances I would have been a therapist, and in a way I am, because what I do is almost always therapeutic for my clients. It helps them to get a different, more positive perspective on what's happening in their lives.

I've discovered that the more I appear on television, the

more comfortable I become with the process, and every time I'm presented with a new challenge, I'm able to rise to the occasion. On the humorous side, however, it seems that each time I'm filming a program outside the studio, something goes wrong with the equipment. The batteries on the camera go dead, or the lights don't work. Not too long ago, I was on an AM radio call-in program when, in the middle of the show, the entire phone system went down. I believe these "failures" are a result of the intensity of the energy emanating from so many souls wanting to come through as well as the intensity of my own energy.

I should also add here that I believe things are thrown in our paths for a reason, so that we are given the opportunity to reach higher and become better. An extreme tragic yet heroic example of this is the way Todd Beamer and his fellow passengers reacted on Flight 93 during the horrific events of 9/11. It was not accidental that those people were on that particular flight and, in their final moments, saved the lives of thousands by making sure the plane did not reach its intended target.

Learn to appreciate the value of the gifts
you've been given.

Another thing that has made me more comfortable is my understanding that however much other people may want to *think* I control what happens in their lives, I really don't. I don't even control what comes into my own life by way of the messages I receive. And whatever I am able to tell my clients, they still are the ones who have to decide what they will do with the information. I don't know what the message is going to mean to the person receiving it, and sometimes I don't even understand the meaning myself. I'm just the conduit, the messenger.

People often ask me how I get my information from souls on the other side, and the best way I can explain it is that most often I see psychic photographs in my mind. The souls show me pictures or symbols or a name or a date that they know will have a distinct meaning to the person they're contacting. So, for example, when I was doing a reading on the radio for someone whose mother's name was Lucille and who had red hair, guess whose picture came into my mind? Of course it was Lucille Ball, and, naturally, the woman I was reading for recognized the meaning of that picture immediately.

But even though I now know I'm not responsible for the messages I receive, I've also learned—since that day I made my teacher cry—that I can't just blurt out whatever comes into my head. I am responsible for what I say, and I need to be very careful how I say it, because what I tell people can, and often does, have a profound effect on their lives. Even though messages from souls on the other side are always delivered out of love, they're not always the messages people on this side want to hear. I try to make all my clients understand that what I'm telling them is intended to help and direct them, but sometimes, unfortunately, they just shut down. They may not want to hear it or they may not know what to do with it, and very often they still want me to tell them what to do.

CHANGING YOUR PATH IS UP TO YOU

Even after all this time it continues to amaze me when I give someone a message and he or she asks me, "Well, what should

I do? Should I do this or that?" All I can say to these people is, "This is what your loved one on the other side is telling me, and you have to make up your own mind how to act on it." I consider myself the facilitator who helps other people to realize that they do have a path and that, if they want to, they can change it. Elisabeth Kübler-Ross, the psychiatrist and well-known writer on death and the afterlife, put it most clearly when she said, "I believe that we are solely responsible for our choices, and we have to accept the consequences of every deed, word, and thought throughout our lifetime." Often, however, people don't want that responsibility. They're afraid that if they make a change, they won't do it right, they'll mess it up in some way, and, therefore, it's easier for them to pass the responsibility on to me. Or, when I tell them as clearly as I know how what their loved one is telling me they should do, they go right out and do the opposite—and still they blame it on me. For example, a young woman came to me recently who had been living with her boyfriend and was having difficulties with the relationship. She had issues with her father, who had passed, and now she was acting out that same relationship all over again. I told her that the spirits were letting me know she should let her boyfriend move out, give him the space to work out his own problems, and then they'd be able to sort out their relationship. Of course, she chose not to listen, and when things didn't go well, she called my office wanting to blame me for the outcome. Some people just want to prove that they can outwit the dead, but, as I've learned over the years, the dead always know more than we do.

Sometimes, though, their message comes through so loud and clear that just receiving it is enough for the person to make significant changes in his or her life.

No psychic can change your life for you.
That's something you've got to do for yourself.

One really dramatic example of this occurred after someone heard me on the radio. This woman had five daughters, and one of them, Donna, was not only in terrible trouble herself but was causing an enormous amount of heartache for her family. She came from a well-to-do family that had always struggled with her father's alcoholism. Now Donna was addicted to crack cocaine and was stealing from her own family to support her habit. It had gotten to the point where her mother and her sisters had to keep all their valuables locked up so that she couldn't get to them. So when the mother heard me, she said that something told her to take a chance. She called to make an appointment and brought Donna to me.

A very attractive woman in her early twenties, Donna was a Debra Winger look-alike with shoulder-length chestnut brown hair and big brown eyes, but I have to say that when she arrived in my office she looked pretty terrible—and she looked even more shaken up when she left. What happened was that Donna's grandmother came through and started telling her not only what was going on in her life at the moment, including identifying the two crackheads she was hanging out with who had stolen the family car, but also where the family plot was, who was going to be at her funeral, and what she was going to be wearing in the casket if she didn't make some big changes in her life. In fact, Donna was on such a self-destructive path that she knew she wouldn't be here much longer and she'd already chosen the dress she wanted to be buried in. When her grand-mother was able to describe it, Donna was shocked. But she also knew that the information I was giving her was valid, and it scared her to the point where she went into a forty-five day rehab program and is now on the path to recovery. Her grandmother was just giving her a heads-up that she was very close to joining her on the other side. Donna could have ignored the message—that was her choice. But she didn't.

Your loved ones in spirit want to help you, so it's a good idea to listen to what they have to say. The choice is yours to make.

Donna's been back to see me since then, and she's still clean, but, as I've told her, her grandma is still warning me that she isn't necessarily over the hump and she needs to do the fol-low-up work in terms of continuing therapy and staying away from her old haunts to make sure she doesn't slip back.

Donna's grandmother loved her so much that she inter-vened, but she couldn't make Donna change. Her granddaughter had to do that for herself. I believe that the grandmother made sure Donna's mother was listening to my radio program that day because she knew I'd be able to deliver her message in a way that would make Donna sit up and take notice.

Interventions of this intensity don't occur all the time, but when they do they have a profound effect. If Donna's grandmother had known that the path she was on was, for whatever reason, the one she was supposed to be following, she couldn't have changed that. But because she knew Donna was straying from her path and causing her family so much pain, she felt it was her duty to come through and intervene. And my duty was to keep my emotions out of it and deliver her message as clearly and directly as I could.

An equally profound intervention occurred when I worked with a woman named Sarah, whose husband, Lew, had suffered from severe bipolar illness. Sarah is a doctor who had helped a lot of people in her work, but, for whatever reason, she and her family had simply chosen to believe that Lew's illness was not as serious as it was—until, one day, he just snapped and shot himself in the head. Now Sarah was distraught because she had two children, a son and a daughter, who had both inherited their father's tendency toward manic depression, and she was terrified that her son, Greg, would also take his own life. During our session, Lew came through and began to show me images of his son involved with photography. Sarah confirmed that Greg had recently begun to show an interest in film and had even asked for a video camera. Lew then made it clear that the boy wasn't planning to become a Hollywood director but was, in fact, videotaping the rehearsal of his own death. He told me there was a tape hidden in a shoe box on a shelf in Greg's closet, which is exactly where Sarah found it after our meeting. Now, because of Lew's intervention, Greg has gotten psychiatric counseling, is taking medication, and is on the road to becoming a successful artist.

IT CAN BE OVERWHELMING

Although I have, over the years, come to love what I do, I don't love having to give people information I know they'd rather not

have. In fact, sometimes the sense of responsibility I feel for saying things just the right way so that people will be willing to listen and really *hear* what I'm telling them can be a bit
overwhelming. I think I've learned to do that pretty well just because I'm so aware of it, and I can generally sense how much a
client will be able to deal with at any one time. But, at the same
time, I realize that people have to learn how to receive what I tell
them. It doesn't do them any good to let their emotions get in
the way, and I also have to make sure I don't let my own emotions interfere with what I'm doing.

I probably shouldn't, but I do sometimes still get hurt
when people tell me I'm "doing the devil's work" or accuse me
of using some kind of trickery. I know that getting upset doesn't
do me any good, but sometimes I just can't help it. I don't try to
make anyone believe in an afterlife or in my ability to communicate with souls in spirit. I don't make them come see me or at-
tend my events or listen to my radio program; I just can't
understand why they'd want to buy a ticket or tune in or call up
just to tell me I'm a fake or, worse, that what I'm doing is somehow evil.

But if I know I shouldn't be angry or upset when people
don't want to hear—or just refuse to believe—what I'm telling
them, I also can't allow myself to become emotionally involved
in other people's pain or to get all puffed up about the positive
changes I can help them to make in their lives.

GETTING EMOTIONAL DOESN'T HELP

One of the worst things that can happen to someone like me is
starting to think of myself as the one who's in charge. I call it the
rock star mentality. To put it another way, I need to keep remem-

bering that I'm not the violinist; I'm the violin. I'm the instrument that's used by those who have passed on to "play their music." I can't make music without them, and the only sounds that come out of me are the ones they want me to make. If I ever lost that sense of who I am and what I'm here for, I'd be straying from my own path, which would be just as bad as trying to run away from it as I did originally.

My work can be extremely emotional. It's up to me to be sure that my emotions don't get in the way and block my senses.

Another problem I have to watch out for is becoming emotionally involved with my clients and their stories or problems. People almost always come to me when they're in trouble or in pain. If they're perfectly happy with the way their lives are going, they're probably not in the frame of mind to start shaking things up by consulting a psychic. To do my job—and I have to keep remembering that it is a job—I need to keep my emotions in check because emotions create a kind of barrier that prevents me from receiving the communications that dead people want me to pass on. Sometimes that's not so easy because I actually feel everything that's coming at me both from my client and from the spirit world. I feel the impact of the client's sadness, the happiness of the message, and even the physical pain of the way the soul who's coming through has passed. If someone died of a head trauma, I feel that trauma; if it was an embolism or a heart attack or a stroke, I feel the emotion and the pain. And sometimes those feelings are so intense that it's difficult to get back to myself when the reading is over.

The time it's hardest to control my emotions is when I'm dealing with a child who has passed, because I'm a parent myself, or when I have a close connection with the person I'm trying to help. When that happens, I just have to take a step back and do what I call a separation of church and state. That can be difficult, but it's something I know I need to do if I'm going to be effective. I remember, for example, when my wife's grandfather was in a coma after suffering a cranial bleed. At the same time, her grandmother felt so guilty about not hearing him and being there to call an ambulance that she suffered a heart attack and was also in the hospital. So when my wife and I went to the hospital to say good-bye to him, I thought the intensity of the emotional circumstances would keep me from connecting with him, but that's not how it went. I knew on a psychic level that he was going to pass the next day, and I sat there that night and reached into myself, telling myself, you know, this isn't about you. It's really about his wanting to release, and we have to help him because he's so concerned about what's going to happen to his wife that he keeps holding on. By telling myself that, I could take myself out of the equation and communicate to him that his wife would be okay and that it was okay for him to go in peace. And he did go the next day.

Remember, It's Not About You

To stay focused on my purpose I have to constantly keep reminding myself that it's not about me—it's never about me. And sometimes the best thing I can do for other people is to help them understand it's not about them either. A good case in point is a woman who came to me after her husband of fifty years had died. She simply couldn't get over the fact that he'd "left" her, and she was completely focused on her own pain and suffering. What she'd lost track of was that her husband, whom she'd clearly loved very much, had been suffering for a very long time and was now not suffering any longer. I was able to let her know not only that her husband was still and would always be a part of her life but also that he was now at peace and no longer in pain and that he wanted her to move past her pain as well.

Wanting to help us move on with our lives and, essentially, continue to follow our own path and learn the lessons we're here for is one of the primary reasons those who've passed over continue to communicate with us. Sometimes, as I've said, the death of a loved one can open a new door in our lives that shows us a new direction and really helps us understand our own purpose for being on this earth. But sometimes it can be such a blow that it completely knocks us off our tracks. And when that happens, we're in real danger of getting stuck.

Everything in life—even death—happens for a reason, but it's sometimes difficult for people to believe that.

When people experience a tragedy, particularly if a loved one dies young, or of a terrible illness, or in an accident, or by violent means, they often need validation that the tragedy they've experienced has a reason, that it isn't just senseless. If these people are able to understand that whoever it is has died because his or her mission here was over or because it was part of the soul's path, they are usually able to come to terms with the loss instead of being permanently derailed by it. Most of the time, I'm able to give them that gift of understanding, as I did Fran following the death of her daughter. I'll let her tell you about it in her own words.

FRAN'S STORY

"I went to see Jeffrey for the first time a few months after my daughter Tabatha was diagnosed with ovarian cancer. What he told me during that initial reading was so gentle and so comforting that he gave me a real sense of peace.

"Then, as my daughter was getting worse—I think it was in late May—my sister called him on my behalf, and he told her to tell me to 'hold on until the middle of July and it will be over with.' When my sister told me that, even though I knew Tabatha was dying, I wanted to believe it meant that she'd be okay. Of course, it didn't mean that at all. Later Jeffrey told my sister that he'd delivered the message the way he did because he didn't have the heart to just spit it right out and tell me.

"Tabatha died on July 15, and she was totally at peace. My husband and I had spent two weeks with her in the hospice, and there was such an overwhelming peace about her the whole time that you could just feel it.

"My last reading with Jeffrey was by telephone. All I wanted then was validation of what I really already knew—that she was okay. I just needed to hear it from her, and I knew I'd hear it from her through him.

"Jeffrey told me that she could have stayed a little bit longer, but my mother and father, who are both on the other side, made it go more quickly because she was suffering so much. She was so vibrant and had so much energy; she was counseling other women with ovarian cancer and their families over the internet, and she just never quit, right up to the end. She was angry, of course, but she was also very protective of me, and she kept a lot of what she was going through to herself.

"Jeffrey told me so many things that day that sounded so much like her, I was laughing and crying at the same time. He told me that I had to get myself together because she was busy over there "checking out the guys," and I was laughing and thinking to myself, that would be just like her, always looking on the bright side and trying to make me feel better. And she was also very adamant about my health. I have a lot of health problems myself, and sometimes I'd ask myself why I was still here when she wasn't. I just wanted to die and be with her. I didn't say any of this to Jeffrey, but he knew what I was thinking, and he told me I was here for a reason. 'You have a family. You have Mr. Wonderful'—which is exactly what my smart-aleck daughter would call my husband—'and if you fall apart, he's going to keep falling apart.' And that was also right on the money because my husband had a small breakdown after Tabatha died. He was hospitalized for a short time, and when he sees I'm not in a good place it affects him. But Jeffrey has never met my husband and he couldn't possibly have known any of this. So Tabatha was telling me I have to take care of myself because I have a family here that needs me. She was a very strong person, and now I have to become a strong person.

"I'd actually been planning to go away and take some

time for myself, which I think is necessary, but then I wound up in the hospital instead. Jeffrey told me that Tabatha said, 'Wherever you were planning to go, you need to go.' All I could say was, 'My God, I was sick in the hospital, give me a break,' and he said, 'Yeah, and it was your own fault because you don't take care of yourself,' which is exactly the way she would have said it.

"So, yes, Tabatha was a little angry with me because I'd promised her that I'd be happy and go on with my life. And I did, but it was difficult. When my daughter was sick, of course I wanted to be in control. I just wanted it to go away, but Jeffrey made me understand I couldn't do that and that I had to get to the point where I accepted that she was okay—and I wasn't. When I hung up the phone that day, I was absolutely on a high because I knew in my heart of hearts that she was okay. I know we'll be together again. I just miss her physically. I'd never been to a psychic before Jeffrey, and for a while I was a little bit scared of the unknown, but now I'm completely open to it."

You Need to Find Your True Path

It's fulfilling for me to know that I could help Fran come to terms with her daughter's passing and understand that she had to continue to follow her own path. That said, however, we humans can be stubborn, and sometimes we just don't want to see what we're supposed to be doing—certainly I'm a prime example of someone who took a few detours before I was willing to acknowledge that none of those side trips was getting me where I knew I was supposed to be going. Yes, we all have free will, but we're really good at making mistakes, and we're also good at repeating our mistakes. We all come into the world with a particular soul purpose, but it can take some people a long time to figure out what that is.

———

As a way of understanding this, we can look at certain public figures and see that some of them "got it" pretty quickly while others had to almost self-destruct before they got on the right path. Bill Gates, for example, was so clear about what he knew he should be doing that he dropped out of college to start what would become the multibillion-dollar Microsoft empire that has effectively revolutionized the whole concept of global communication. But then we can look at someone like Darryl Strawberry, an extraordinarily gifted athlete who wound up following such a self-destructive path that he almost died twice—once from addiction and once from colon cancer—before he was able to turn his life around.

> We humans make a lot of mistakes. It can
> take us a long time to "get with the program"
> and figure out what we really should be doing
> to find fulfillment for ourselves.

To me this means that we can have a great soul purpose and just not be able to handle it. However, when and if we do manage to get on the right track, we'll feel fulfilled by what we're doing. When people achieve greatness, it's because they've found their true path. But don't get me wrong. I don't mean that if you haven't achieved "greatness" you're on the wrong path. Not every one of us is going to do something that puts us in the public spotlight or creates dramatic change in the world. What I mean is that once we figure out what's right for us and go with it, we'll be at peace with ourselves and with whatever comes our way. Although we sometimes hear about people who find their path and rise to greatness, fulfillment also comes in less obvious, more personal terms. To quote Elisabeth Kübler-Ross one more time, "As far as service goes, it can take the form of a million things. To do service, you don't have to be a doctor working in the slums for free, or become a social worker. Your position in life and what you do doesn't matter as much as how you do what you do."

Having said that, however, I should also say that if you've been getting knocked around, if things haven't been working out for you, you shouldn't be beating yourself up about it because that, too, is part of your path. It's just that the road is bumpier for some of us than it is for others. The way I look at it is that some of us have harder heads than others so it takes a while longer to knock some sense into us.

IT'S NOT ALWAYS SMOOTH SAILING, BUT IT'S ALWAYS UP TO YOU

The bottom line is that we still have free will. That's a hard concept for some people to grasp: We're put here with a purpose, but it's up to us whether we make it easy or hard for ourselves to get in line with what we're supposed to be doing. Some of us don't like to think it's up to us. That's what I meant when I talked about people who wanted to hand me control of their lives by getting me to make their decisions for them. When things are going great, we're happy enough to take responsibility for our successes, but when things aren't working out for us, we'd like to blame anyone and anything but ourselves and the choices we make. Well, I'm sorry to have to tell you this, but to paraphrase the words of Harry Truman, the buck stops with you.

If you take credit for your successes, you also
need to credit yourself for whatever's going
wrong in your life.

Energy is a constant—it's in us and all around us. We create bad energy for ourselves by making bad decisions, and the learning process is to take the energy in our life and make it work for us. I believe that one of the biggest struggles most of us have is understanding how to turn a bad situation into a good one. When we remain stuck in a negative pattern, we're putting ourselves in our own way. It can take us a long time to learn because we're the ones holding things up.

Yes, I believe there's a higher power, but that belief in no way negates my belief in free will. In fact, I don't see how you can believe in an afterlife and not believe in a higher power. And, conversely, how can you believe in the concept of heaven and not accept the existence of a spirit world?

To me the higher power is a voice in my head directing me. People sometimes ask me how I can trust the source of that inner voice, and all I can say is it's so distinct that I know it's coming from somewhere beyond my own ego. As I explained in the note to my readers at the beginning of this book, I have been exposed to a variety of faiths, and my way of experiencing a connection with the higher power is very personal, as it is for everyone. Some people believe you have to go to church and follow the tenets of a particular religion, and there's nothing I do that conflicts with that. Personally, however, I believe the higher power incorporates all the practices and beliefs of all the different religions. I burn incense in my office to be sure that there is no residual negative soul energy hanging around. I use holy water to cleanse a particular location of bad energy when I think that's called for. And I believe very strongly in honoring the dead by lighting a candle as is customary in the Jewish religion.

I do go to church, and I find it comforting, but for me the more important thing is making that everyday connection, which I do through prayer. I pray every morning before I begin my work, because doing that raises my spiritual vibrations and gets me ready for whatever the day will bring. Sometimes I pray to St. Anthony or St. Jude, but, as I said, how you pray or direct your prayers isn't really what matters. Everyone has to determine what's comfortable for him or her. It could be prayer or meditation or even just taking a quiet moment to assess your goals and ask for whatever it is you want to come into your life.

Different religions use chanting as a way to raise spiritual vibrations—Buddhists chant *ohm,* Jews chant readings from the Torah, Roman Catholics say the rosary—but however you choose to do it, by connecting with that vibration you're expanding what I like to call your soul presence and bringing a better energy into your life. Often, when I meet a spiritual person, I can see it in his or her aura, which might be gold or purple or sometimes a bright white light.

Do you believe in a higher power?
How do you define it for yourself?
How do you think this higher power can help
you in your daily life?

If I had to describe how I define my sense of the higher power, I'd say it's a soul that's evolved from us, a higher consciousness that doesn't interfere in our process but is there to offer spiritual support. That higher power has put us here for a reason, but it's up to us to figure out what that reason is and accept it. Being unwilling or unable to figure that out—what I like to call getting in our own way—is my definition of hell.

Let's say, for example, you're in one business after another and your businesses keep failing. If you keep failing, you're probably not happy, and maybe you ought to take that as a sign that you ought to be doing something else. Or maybe you're just afraid to take responsibility for your own business decisions, so you're letting someone else make them for you. If that's the case, you're handing over control of your life, but you're doing it of your own free will. Any way you look at it, you've still got free will. You may not be able to control everything that comes at you in life, but you can control how you see it and react to it.

If you can't get out of your own way, you're
creating your own version of hell on earth.

In my own case, I still can't control the psychic communications I receive or the messages I get from the spirit world, but I can choose how I react to them. At first I chose to fight them, ignore them when I could, and hide them when I couldn't. Eventually, however, I realized that was never going to make me happy or fulfilled. It took a lot of bumping and nudging from the other side to get me to acknowledge my true purpose, but in the end, the decision was still mine to make.

Once you understand that your life has a reason and a purpose, you'll find it easier to tune in to the signs that let you know whether you're headed in the right direction. Although it's become a cliché to talk about how the tragedy of 9/11 acted as a wake-up call for people all over the world, I have to say that I think it was an event of such monumental impact that it's actually helped us to evolve as souls. Another such cataclysmic disaster was the tsunami of December 2004. When we're made aware of how dramatically life can change in an instant, we're literally shaken out of our complacency and we can't help paying more attention to what we as individuals are doing with our lives every day. Suddenly we become aware of how important it is for us to actively seek happiness and purpose instead of just drifting along and assuming there will always be another chance to do it differently tomorrow. To me that means we're coming closer to understanding our soul purpose.

I believe that we're all meant to connect with other souls in some way and that those who have passed are very good at helping us to make those connections. It's just up to us to accept the help they keep offering. In my own case, I had to help myself work through my own denial before I could accept my gift and use it to connect with others so that they, too, could connect with the souls who would help them.

SOUL PRINTS

❋ Don't run away from the gifts you've been given.

❋ Discovering your path can change your life.

❋ Stop questioning the higher power, the voice from within.

❋ Those in spirit can help put you on the right path—but only if you're willing to listen.

❋ Our loved ones in spirit communicate because they want to help us move on.

❋ The death of a loved one can help you to find your true path.

❋ Some people are really stubborn—they can be their own worst enemies.

❋ Once you understand your life has a purpose, it will be easier for you to tune in to the signs.

❋ Make prayers and goals a part of your life.

2

What the Spirit World Has Taught Me About Life

Probably the most important and powerful lesson the world of spirit has taught me is just how much work they're doing "behind the scenes" to prompt us as we play out our lives. From subtle whispers to psychic screams, they're constantly doing whatever they think is necessary to connect us with one another and with our own life's purpose. Like all loved ones, they want us to do well. And, in most cases, fear is the only thing that's preventing us from listening to what they're trying to tell us and living as rich and full a life as we should and can be.

A Therapist Talks About Fear

Dr. Jane Greer is a classically trained psychotherapist and author of *The Afterlife Connection*. In her book, Dr. Greer explains that she had always been open to the possibility of life after death but began to make her own connections only after her beloved mother died in 1998. When I asked her to talk about the therapist's view of where fear comes from and how it can hold people back, she explained that fear is an expression of loss. "To do something new," she said, "you have to let go of something familiar and safe, and the minute you do that you become frightened and anxious about whether what you'll get to replace it will be as good or better than what you had." She went on to say that even though doing something new is an opportunity, most people get caught up in what they won't have anymore rather than in the excitement of what they will get. The anxiety overpowers the excitement. It's a question of "the devil you know as opposed to the devil you don't know."

In terms of fearing the future, Dr. Greer believes that people are afraid it might be worse than their current situation, and this fear can prevent them from wanting to know about it. "Some people are afraid to consult a psychic," she said, "because they look on it as a loss of free will. They think everything is fated, ergo potentially fateful in a negative way. That, in turn, makes them feel powerless rather than empowered to face and overcome obstacles, because they believe it's all preordained anyway."

And when it comes to fear of death, well, that's the biggest unknown of all—playing for the highest stakes—and also the greatest loss. "People don't know what to expect and, therefore, they don't know how to manage it," Dr. Greer concludes.

WHAT THE SPIRITS HAVE TAUGHT ME ABOUT FEAR

It's interesting but probably not so surprising that virtually everything she told me agrees with what I've learned and experienced myself. It's usually fear that prevents people from taking the leap of letting go so that they can grab on to something better for themselves. And, as I've already discussed, it's the mistaken belief that someone like me or some power in the world of spirit has control of their future that causes people to want to abdicate and give up responsibility for their own choices. But that, of course, isn't true.

If you're not happy, if you're not getting what you want or need in life, why not try to change? What have you really got to be afraid of?

It's the spirits themselves who taught me that everything we experience in our lives happens for a reason, and that, at the same time, we always have a choice about how we respond to our experiences. Here's an example of how fear can prevent us from making the choices that will allow us to follow our true path, and how persistent the spirits can be about putting us back on track.

Roberta was an actress who appeared to be just on the brink of becoming very successful, but instead of pushing herself to reach the next level, each time an opportunity came up for her, such as going to an audition or having to decide whether or not to take a particular role, she would hesitate or second-guess herself because she was simply afraid to take the next step. She could never just let herself "go for it" because she was always afraid of making a mistake. It was almost as if she were purposely trying to sabotage herself. But no matter how often she did that, she kept running into people who could help move her career forward, and new opportunities continued to open up. I explained to her that these weren't accidents, she wasn't just "lucky," there was energy coming at her from the spirit world that was constantly trying to let her know what she was supposed to be doing until finally Roberta was able to accept that this really was her true path. In this particular case, it was her grandmother, Lois, who had been in vaudeville and knew her granddaughter had the talent to succeed, who had been acting as her spirit guide and directing her until she was able to believe in herself and make it happen.

WE MAKE OUR OWN BAD LUCK

Whatever you may think, there truly is no such thing as good luck or bad luck. In reality, we create our own "bad luck" by running away from whatever it is that would make us happy. And so, if like Roberta you find that you're constantly being pushed in a direction you're trying to avoid because you're afraid of some imagined disaster just around the next corner, that's exactly the time to stop and consider *why* you're being so negative and what lesson you're supposed to be learning. In other words, let your fear be a wake-up call and try to understand how you can make it work for you. Is what you're doing making you happy? Do you feel that your life has a purpose? What's the worst thing that could happen if you did something different? If you could do whatever it is you're afraid of, do you think you'd be happier?

"To conquer fear is the beginning of wisdom."
—*Bertrand Russell*

Remember that the spirit world operates on pure energy, like the current running through an appliance. When fear gets in the way and stops us cold, it's like shorting out the appliance. But the spiritual current is still there, and if we can just push through our fear and hit the reset button, we'll be reconnected and the energy will start flowing again.

"Good luck," then, is being able to change bad or negative energy to the positive and make it work to our advantage, but most people just don't know how to do that. I get really irritated when people tell me, "Oh, Jeffrey, I'm just not lucky." Luck, I tell them, is like the law of karma—whatever you put out, you get back, or, to put it another way, what goes around comes around. Every event or situation creates another event or situation. You can choose to keep doing the same thing, putting out what you've always been putting out, and perpetuate your bad luck. Or you can change the energy you put out and get back something new and more positive.

"What we call luck is the inner man externalized. We make things happen to us."

—*Robertson Davies*

I'm not saying that we should be totally naïve and walk around with our head in the clouds assuming that everyone is good and means well, or that things will just "work out" without our having to work for them. But, on the other hand, we don't need to be walking around like the *Peanuts* character with a perpetual rain cloud over his head. We have the ability to manipulate the kind of energy we put out so that we also change what comes back to us.

LET FEAR BE YOUR MOTIVATOR

As I've said, when we're really afraid of something, we should probably start to think about how we can use that fear as a motivator. I realized that for myself when I faced my fear of putting myself out in the world as a psychic by going on television. Once I did it, I discovered that I was actually very good at it. Instead of being terrified, as I had feared, I was totally relaxed. I loved it, and that turned out to be a great adrenaline rush. As a result, I didn't get rid of just that particular fear, I got rid of the whole idea that I ever needed to be afraid of anything again. It's amazing how quickly fear evaporates when we see how unnecessary it was for us to have been afraid in the first place.

> Consider that the thing you're most afraid of might be exactly what you ought to be seeking or doing. Maybe you're afraid because you want it so much. You'll never know until you take that leap of faith and go for it.

That's not the same as giving yourself up to fate or saying what the heck, whatever will be will be. That would be denying your gift of free will, and I don't ever do that. Instead I accept the fact that allowing fear to rule my life would be failing to use the free will I've been given. If you can understand fear in that context, you'll be able to see that your fear isn't keeping you safe—it's actually preventing you from reaching fulfillment.

"Fear of trying causes paralysis. Trying causes
only trembling and sweating."

—*Mason Cooley*

CLIMBING THE TREE OF LIFE

In terms of reaching fulfillment, my personal belief is that the reason for the continuation of soul consciousness is for us to continue our journey and to grow, and in order to do that the soul must also reincarnate.

I like to describe the process of reincarnation by saying that no soul ever goes to waste, it just keeps getting recycled in new and different forms. I know that might sound to you like using up the leftovers from the Thanksgiving turkey, but it isn't. It's more like a constant renewal of the tree of life. Almost every culture in the world has some representation of the tree of life. With roots in the earth and branches reaching to the heavens, the tree represents spiritual growth, the joining of those here on earth with some kind of higher power or consciousness. And because most trees shed their leaves and temporarily "die" in the winter, then come back into bloom and are "reborn" in the spring, they symbolize eternal regeneration. To me, this is the best way to describe what happens as souls reincarnate to grow and develop and come closer and closer to fulfilling their purpose.

In terms of organized religion, my belief is closest to that of Buddhism, which teaches that people do not live and die just once but are reborn a number of times before reaching what they call nirvana. Nirvana is not a place, as Christians visualize a heaven, but rather a state of being that occurs when someone no longer has desires that promote selfish attitudes and has, therefore, arrived at enlightenment.

Although both Judaism and Christianity also believe in the survival of the soul, their view of what happens to the soul after death seems to be much more overtly judgmental. The Torah indicates in several places that the righteous will be reunited with their loved ones after death while the wicked will be excluded from this happy family reunion. Resurrection of the dead will occur only when the Messiah arrives to usher in a perfect world of peace and prosperity, at which time the righteous will be brought back to life and the wicked will not.

This teaching can be compared to the Christian Day of Judgment, when Christ will come to judge the living and the dead. Until that time, individuals are consigned after death to heaven, hell, or purgatory, according to how they lived their lives. Interestingly, however, Pope John Paul II is quoted in a 1998 article in the German journal *Bild* as having told a group of pilgrims that

> One should not think life begins after death only with the final judgment. Quite special conditions prevail after death. It concerns a transitional phase in which the body dissolves and where the life of a mirror-image entity (the soul) begins.
>
> This entity is equipped with its own conscious-

ness and its own will, so that humans exist, although they no longer possess a physical body.

One thing I have learned through my ongoing communication with the world of spirit is that souls go to the other side and stay there until they are ready or need to come back. Some take a long time until they're ready to come back; others need to return more quickly—but quickly, in terms of the soul, is at least eighty to one hundred years. (Animals, as I'll be discussing in the following chapter, return more quickly because they don't have the same kinds of issues to work out as humans do. And the same is true of babies who, as I'll be explaining, may come into the wrong body, go out quickly, and then come back more quickly.) Ultimately, however, the soul needs to reincarnate in order to evolve, and then, after several reincarnations, it may evolve to a level where it doesn't need to come back anymore, and those souls then move on to the next level in the world of spirit.

WHY ARE WE AFRAID?

When I think about where fear comes from, I believe that most often it's connected to a past-life experience or to past traumas in this life. For instance, a woman was agoraphobic and terrified of being buried alive, and I was able to tap into her past-life experiences. I discovered that in a previous life she'd been a slave who was buried in a cave. Then, in this life, when she was a child her brother used to lock her in the closet, which brought back all her past-life fears of dark, enclosed spaces. It was dark in the closet and she felt she couldn't breathe, but until I was able to see into her past life and discover the reason, she had no idea why she was reacting so traumatically. In another case, a woman's husband, a judge, was obsessively concerned about issues of ethics. In this instance I was able to discover that in a past life he'd been in a situation where he was removed from office.

So I do believe that we are deeply influenced by past experiences we're not even aware of. Very often when I'm working with people, I'm able to get a sense of what I like to call their road map—the map or path their soul is intended to follow that is tied into where their soul is in its evolution, which in turn is determined by the experiences they've had or the lessons they've learned in past incarnations. By doing that I'm often able to clarify where they are in their soul path and where they should be going.

But most people don't want to or simply can't make the connection between their present fear and where it might have originated. Instead they just use fear as an excuse because they're so paralyzed by it that they can't see past it to what they're supposed to be doing. Fear is what causes us to keep making the same mistakes over and over instead of moving forward, which is why we keep reincarnating until we get it right.

PUSH THROUGH YOUR FEAR
AND THE ENERGY WILL FLOW

A perfect example of how fear can prevent us from following our true path was brought home to me when I worked with Don, a young man whose father and grandfather had both held good, lucrative jobs as members of the electricians' union. Don's grandfather had been so influential in convincing his father to follow in his footsteps and become a member of the union that the father, in turn, was imposing those beliefs on his own son. When Don expressed an interest in going to college, his father had persuaded him that he wasn't smart enough, that he shouldn't even be thinking of going that route, and that he, too, should be following the family's tradition of joining a union.

I was able to show Don that his grandfather had imposed these beliefs on his father, who was now passing that influence on to him. Once he understood that his fear of breaking the pattern had no validity for his own life, he was able to move past his fear. Without the information I was able to give him, however, he would have been far less likely to recognize where the beliefs that his father and grandfather were handing down to him had come from. He would almost certainly have followed in his father's and grandfather's footsteps, and for Don that would have meant never experiencing the fulfillment to be gained by following his own true path. As it was, he did go to college and then to law school, and he is now a thriving tax attorney and a certified public accountant.

> Think of all the negative energy you're expending on your fears. Imagine how much positive energy you'd have if you just let go of those fears.

In a similar situation I met a woman named Edith who had been a stay-at-home mom for many years. She'd gone to college and had dreamed of becoming an attorney, but she married young, became pregnant, and gave up her ambition.

She'd been afraid that if she postponed having children she'd miss out on the opportunity ever to be a mother, but when I was able to connect with her grandfather, who had also been a lawyer, I realized what her real road had been all along and was able to convince her that she needed to get back on track. As a result, she did go back to school and today she is a very successful attorney.

And finally, there was Christina, a bright young woman studying to be a doctor who had been to three different colleges and managed, each time she was on the brink of completing her courses, to self-destruct. When she came to see me, her mother came through and explained the family history. It seemed that Christina's maternal grandfather had been a prestigious physician, and his daughter—Christina's mother—had been destined to follow in his footsteps. Unfortunately, however, the pressure for her to succeed was so great that she was never able to pass her medical boards and eventually became a suicide. Now she could see that her daughter was in danger of following the same path. With the information she gave me, however, I was able to persuade Christina to see a therapist, who was able, in turn, to help her understand that her unconscious fear of failure was preventing her from fulfilling her true potential. Because of the help she received, Christina is now a cardiothoracic fellow in pediatrics.

MAKING THE RIGHT CONNECTIONS

For us on earth, however, to move forward or not is always a choice, and the spirit world is very good at getting us to make the connections that will help us make the right choice. If our dead loved ones feel they need to get a message to us, they'll make it happen, and one way they do that is by putting us in touch with the right people. Not surprisingly, because of the work I do, that person very often is me. I absolutely believe the spirits arrange for who gets to see me, and the ones who were pushy in life remain equally pushy on the other side. I can't tell you how often someone who is unable to keep an appointment with me sends someone else who receives an urgent message. But even when I'm not officially "on duty," so to speak, I meet people on vacation or at social events who just happen to have lost someone. Strange (or maybe not so strange) things happen, such as the night I was at a dinner party with my wife, wearing an unusual Ralph Lauren Polo shirt that I normally wouldn't have worn. I didn't know why I'd chosen to put it on that evening, but at dinner I sat next to a woman I'd never met who'd recently lost her husband and who told me that I was wearing her husband's favorite shirt.

Other times, I've been on a plane and have found myself receiving a message for the person sitting next to me. This can sometimes get a little touchy, as I first have to make my seatmate feel comfortable enough to listen to what I know I'm supposed to be telling him or her instead of just freaking out. Usually, I try to have a brief conversation first so that I can explain the work I do, and sometimes I give the person a copy of my book. Then, once I feel that he or she is receptive, I pass along what the spirits are telling me.

Very often I'm just walking down the street or going about my everyday business when I feel a soul literally pulling me toward a total stranger because he or she is so eager to get a message across. I always know whom the message is for because, just as when I do a group event with several hundred people in the room, I'm drawn, as if by an invisible umbilical cord, to a particular person. Admittedly, this can be a touchy situation. After all, what would you think if some guy suddenly walked up to you on the street to deliver an urgent message from your dead grandmother? And it can make doing the grocery shopping rather complicated when I see a soul peering over the shoulder of the woman behind the checkout counter. I've just had to learn to deal with these situations and to handle them as gracefully and tactfully as I can.

Also, whenever I do a group reading or a book signing, there's always someone who tells me he or she just "happened" to be there. Sometimes the person was handed a ticket by a friend who couldn't make it, but I know he or she was being guided by spiritual energy. It's happened time and again.

Life is not full of coincidences. It's full of spirits helping us to make the right connections.

When I do a group event, there may be six or seven hundred people in the room, and more often than not at least one of the people in the audience who receives an important message is someone who "wasn't supposed to be there." For example, at an event that took place on the day after Super Bowl Sunday, one gentleman told me he'd had no intention of coming but had been talked into it by a friend the day before while they were watching the football game. Of course, he got a very clear message from his grandmother that was so specific and came as such a surprise that it completely changed his attitude toward the whole concept of life after death and our ability to communicate with those in spirit. The experience actually opened his mind to a belief he never would have been able to accept had he not been there to "see it for himself."

I often receive emails from people who tell me they "just happened" to be in a bookstore and picked up my book "by accident," and I have to laugh every time that happens. In Fort Myers, Florida, for example, a couple came into the Barnes & Noble bookstore where I was doing a signing, and when they stepped up to the table for me to autograph their copy of my previous book, they told me they'd just "felt the urge" to buy a book that day. As it happened, their son had recently died, and there was a family crisis about which the couple needed information only he could give them. I know that their son guided them to me so that I'd be able to pass them the message he knew they needed to have.

Then, at yet another signing, a woman came up to the table and I knew immediately, even though she didn't tell me, that her mother had recently died. I told her that her mother was showing me a bouquet of pink roses, and as it turned out, her mother loved pink roses and she herself had just planted a pink rosebush. Needless to say, she was amazed by what I'd told her, and she confided that she'd been visiting her mother in the hospital and had just left the room when she died. She'd been feeling very guilty about that, and I explained that her mother's showing her the pink roses was her way of alleviating her daughter's guilt and helping her to get past her grief.

I was also able to let her know that it's not unusual for

people to pass just when a loved one has left the room. The reason is that they're so worried about how we're going to feel when they're gone that we actually hold them back, and it's only when we leave that they're finally able to let go. I told this woman that her mother had put her in my path and that she had actually been meant to leave the room when she did because her mother needed her to do that so she could pass over.

The spirit world was delivering several lessons that day. First, that our loved ones don't really leave us when they move on; second, that when they think we need to hear from them they will find a way to get their message through; and third, that they are at peace and don't want us to feel guilty about something we may have done or not done over which we had no control.

SOUL MATES, CELLMATES, AND EVERYONE IN BETWEEN

I've already talked about how profoundly the death of a loved one can change the trajectory of one's life, but our lives are also inevitably changed, one way or another, by the people with whom we share them on earth. What the spirits have taught me is that those with whom we cross paths always come into our lives for a reason. And don't think the spirits aren't involved in those meetings, too.

You know the lyrics from the Rodgers and Hammerstein song "Hello, Young Lovers": "You fly down the street on the chance that you'll meet, and you meet—not really by chance." Well, it's not just in songs that people meet "not really by chance." Take Beth, the widow of a stockbroker who died in the Twin Towers. Shortly after losing her husband, she was at a social event where she "ran into" Robert, a former boyfriend she hadn't seen in twenty years who, "coincidentally," had just lost his wife. How could I not believe that their spouses in the world of spirit had been arranging that meeting?

Or consider Louise, who as a teenager had been dating Charlie. Charlie then fathered a child with another woman and died in a car accident at the age of nineteen without ever meeting his son. Subsequently, Louise married Charlie's best friend and had three children of her own. Many years later, Louise's eldest daughter married Charlie's son. It wasn't until after the marriage, when Louise started to learn more about her son-in-law's background, that she realized who his father had been. How pleased do you think Charlie was to see the results of his matchmaking talents from the world of spirit?

Sometimes we do meet our soul mate, the person with whom we were meant to spend the rest of our life, but sometimes people come into our life at a particular point for a particular reason, and once they've served that purpose, they leave. I know that sounds a lot like, "Oh, he [or she] is just using you," but that's not what I mean—or not exactly. People do use us and we use them because we need to learn some lesson from one another. A perfect example of how this happens is the story of Linda. Soon after she was divorced, Linda began a relationship with a man who was able to let her experience her true sexuality and recognize the potential her husband had been preventing her from realizing for so many years. But their relationship didn't last. The man broke it off when he realized that he just wasn't prepared to make any kind of commitment to a long-term relationship. Linda, however, had by that time evolved to arrive at a new sense of herself. And although I never met the gentleman in question, I'd be willing to bet that she had taught him something he may not previously have recognized about himself as well. We often hear the conventional wisdom that you never stay with the person you meet on the rebound, but there's a reason for that, because the person plays a role in our being able to move beyond our previous experience so that we can have a better experience in the future.

If you stop to think about it, how many lessons have you learned from people you didn't necessarily get along with or want to spend time with? Even the boss from hell can teach you something about yourself and what you really need to be doing with your life.

So even temporary relationships always have a higher purpose, which is to move us closer to the path our soul is meant to follow. If you try to keep in mind that everything that comes into your life—including people—is put there for a reason, this will begin to make more sense, and maybe you'll even begin to think about what you might have learned from people you wish you'd *never* met.

I like to call those people cellmates because it can sometimes feel as if you're locked in a prison cell with them. If you've known a cellmate you originally mistook for a soul mate, you need to remember first of all that he or she was put in your path for a reason and, second, that if you chose to be with that person, you made that choice of your own free will. So what can you learn from this?

Clearly you made a mistake, but even mistakes have a purpose. Unless we're totally clueless, they ought to teach us something about ourselves. Let's say that your parents had an unhappy marriage and you marry someone who is just like your father. You think this person is your soul mate, but at some point you might come to realize that your mother never got to use the gifts she'd been given and that you are now reliving her life. Very often I've been able to make people aware that just because they made a mistake and married the wrong person, they can still be successful—they can still change their life. Many people believe that because at some point they made a bad decision and got into a bad relationship, they're now stuck. But that isn't true. Whether you stay in the relationship or not, you can change your life once you're able to overcome your fear or whatever is holding you back. Just as no soul goes to waste, so, too, every relationship has a purpose.

Saying that we ought to learn from our mistakes isn't just a cliché—it's a profound lesson in life.

Sometimes, in fact, your so-called cellmate may be put in your path specifically to provide the opportunity for you to change. That's what happened to Sandra. She married a man who turned out to be gay and was leading a double life, having secret assignations with men. One of his partners infected him with the AIDS virus, and after he died Sandra's entire life changed. She became a successful businesswoman and is now fulfilling the potential she'd been unable to achieve while her husband was alive. This may be an extreme example, but it reinforces my belief that everyone with whom our lives intersect is there because of the lessons we have to learn from them or the effect they will have on our own road map.

Cellmates can be friends, lovers, spouses, or relatives, and if we are able to resolve the issues, misconceptions, and differences that make living with them seem like a constant uphill battle, we'll have gone a long way toward finding our own path to fulfillment. If not—if we're too stubborn to learn from our mistake—we may find ourselves repeating that bad relationship until we get it through our thick skulls that we really need to figure out what we've been doing wrong and why we've been doing it.

It's true that it's never too late to learn—which is why no soul goes to waste—but the sooner we're able to resolve the problems that are preventing us from achieving our soul's purpose, the happier and more fulfilled we will be. It may be that we need to let go of our cellmates—if, for instance, they're supposed to be friends but are holding us back rather than providing positive energy—but if they're family members, it is a good idea to try to find a way to make peace with them sooner rather than later.

GET IT RESOLVED OR RISK GETTING STUCK

One of the biggest things I've learned from my contact with the spirit world is that not resolving differences with loved ones here on earth is one of the surest ways for us to get stuck after they've passed. The one in spirit doesn't want to continue the argument from the other side, and he or she will try to get the message through that it's time to make peace, but we here can find that more of a problem as we continue to kick ourselves and beat ourselves up for something we said or did in the past.

Anger is a negative emotion that can hold you
back just as much as fear.

If, on the other hand, we believe that the person who's gone is responsible for having harmed us, we can carry that grudge long after, from his or her point of view, it's "dead and gone." Either way, this unfinished business means that lingering energy is going to be preventing us from moving on with our own lives.

I saw this for myself when Margaret and Elizabeth came to me for a reading after their mother had passed. Because Margaret was still angry with her mother for—as she perceived it—her preference for Elizabeth, she was now transferring her anger to her sister, and because of that they were both having a hard time moving beyond all the anger and coming to peace with their mother's death. Because their mother never liked Margaret's husband, Margaret had always felt that she was left out and excluded from the family circle. Her mother was a very controlling woman, and because Margaret's husband continuously resisted her efforts to control him, she'd kept her distance from both of them. During our reading the mother came through, and although she remained argumentative even in spirit, she did finally admit that Margaret was right and that her treatment had been unfair. Her being able to do that allowed Margaret to let go of her own anger so that she could resolve her difficulties with her sister as well as her mother, and both she and Elizabeth could move beyond the place where they'd been stuck.

In another, even more extreme case, I did a reading for a woman whose father had molested her when she was a child. She came to me because she wanted to contact her mother, but, of course, it was her father who immediately came through. The session became extremely emotional because he apologized profusely for everything he did and didn't do when he was alive. My client began telling me that she didn't want to hear what he had to say, and I had to let her know that until she dealt with him, he wasn't going to go away. In the end, the session was extremely cathartic for her because she was finally able to cry and let go of her anger. Until that moment, even though she was a successful professional with equally successful children and even grandchildren, her life was, on some level, being driven by something that had happened in her childhood.

DEATH IS NEVER ACCIDENTAL

Another way we can be held back is if we have survivor's guilt because we think we should have been the one to go or that we could have prevented the death of a loved one. But, as I've said, everything that comes into our life—including death—is part of our soul's path. Seen from the point of view of the world of spirit, there are no accidental deaths. In fact, it has been my experience that souls almost always know when it's their time to cross over. They let us know in their words, their actions, and their situations, but we sometimes don't want to recognize the signals they're sending us.

Learn to let go of your guilt along with your
anger and your fear.

On the other hand, I'm sure you've heard stories about
near-death experiences where people go to the light and are sent
back because it wasn't their time. One reason I know these stories to be true is that I've personally seen instances when, by any
rational standard we could apply, someone should have died and
didn't. Two of the most dramatic of these instances involved
teenagers who were in terrible automobile accidents. On both of
these occasions, I saw the cars afterward, and they were totally
crushed like empty soda cans someone had stomped with a
heavy boot. And yet, both times the kid walked away unharmed.
There was a spiritual intervention, in one case by the child's father and in the other by the grandfather, because these kids were
not meant to pass at that time.

Sometimes, however, the spirits can intervene to keep us
here in subtler ways—by putting obstacles in our path or by
sending us a psychic message that we might think of as a gut feeling or just the uneasy sense that something isn't going to work
out the way we want it to or think it should.

While I was just finishing this book, I heard about one
of those interfering spirits from Judith, an analyst with a large
brokerage firm who traveled regularly to London on business.
On this particular occasion, however, Judith couldn't seem to get
there. Her first flight was canceled, her next flight was overbooked,
and then, the night before she was finally supposed to leave, she
had a dream in which her grandmother came to her and said,

"You can't go. There's danger." And sure enough, the London terrorist bombings occurred the next day.

Uneasiness and gut feelings are, however, another issue. There are plenty of stories about animals who seem to know when an earthquake or natural disaster is about to occur and run for safety. Scientists often attribute this to their sensing a change in barometric pressure, but I believe they have a keener psychic ability than most people, simply because they don't have an ego-driven consciousness to make them rationalize away what they feel coming at them from the spirit realm. I'll be talking much more about animals in Chapter 4, but I bring this up now to emphasize the fact that we, too, need to heed those feelings beyond rational thought that may be guiding us to safety.

I'm always getting these "jolts" of intuition that are spiritually generated, and sometimes, stubborn guy that I am, I try to test them. For example, as I was driving to a speaking engagement not so long ago, I suddenly heard a voice in my head saying, "Don't get on that highway. There's been a major accident and you're going to be late." Of course, I got on the highway anyway and ran into so much traffic that I barely made it to the place on time.

On another occasion I was doing some handyman work around the house when the little voice in my head said, "Be careful! Maybe you should hire someone. This is not your line of work." And, needless to say, I cut myself badly.

One client who did listen to her gut and probably saved not only her own life but the lives of her entire family actually canceled a scheduled vacation in Indonesia because, as she told me, she just didn't feel good about it. I wasn't as surprised as she was when I learned that, had they gone, they would have been staying at one of the major resorts where the tsunami of December, 2004 made a direct hit.

On another occasion, a client was scheduled to take a train to Washington on business, but for some reason she was wavering about whether or not she wouldn't be better off flying. As she later told it to me, she kept asking herself why she was taking the train. Her inner dialogue went something like, "Why am I doing this? I hate trains. I could take the shuttle and get there much faster." And so on, until she'd delayed so long that she actually missed the train, which subsequently derailed, killing a number of passengers and injuring many more.

If you have a strong sense of uneasiness, it may be your higher, psychic intelligence trying to tell you something.

And in yet another instance I'd been working with a client to try to teach her how to tap in to her inner voice and listen to her gut. One evening, when she went into the city to meet friends, she was walking to the restaurant when, she said, something kept telling her not to walk down a particular street. On this occasion she apparently decided to forget everything we'd been working on because she turned the corner anyway and, as a result, she was mugged.

By Helping Us They Help Themselves

One enlightening perception to be taken from all these stories is that the world of spirit is a beehive of activity. It might seem that all the pushing and prodding, guiding, intervening, and endless caring the spirits do on our behalf wouldn't leave them much time to do the soul work they need to complete before reincarnating, but, as I'll be discussing in the following chapter, their growth and ours remain intertwined because helping us down here is part of their growth up there. As we grow, so do they.

SOUL PRINTS

- ✳ Those in spirit are constantly prompting us from the wings.
- ✳ The spirits are very good at making the right connections with the living.
- ✳ Fear is the thing that most often holds us back from finding or fulfilling our soul's purpose.
- ✳ Fear prevents us from letting go of the known—even if we're not happy with it—so that we can grab on to something better.
- ✳ Fear can be a great motivator.
- ✳ Fear can be connected to past traumas in this life or to a past-life experience.
- ✳ Everything in life happens for a reason.
- ✳ We connect with other people for a reason—because of the lessons we have to teach one another.
- ✳ Even "cellmates" can help us to evolve.
- ✳ We're all responsible for the choices we make.
- ✳ We make our own luck—the bad as well as the good.
- ✳ We continue to reincarnate in order to grow and develop.
- ✳ Resolve your differences with loved ones while they're in this life or risk getting stuck when they pass.
- ✳ Helping us to grow is a way for our loved ones in spirit to evolve.

3

What the Spirits Have Taught Me About Death

The medical definition of death is very simple: When your brain stops functioning, your other organs stop working, and the body dies. But the medical definition doesn't take into account what physics has taught us about energy—that it never dies. It just keeps changing forms. It's that eternally mutable energy we call the soul, and the soul never dies.

"I am a soul. I know well that what I shall render up to the grave is not myself. That which is myself will go elsewhere."

—*Victor Hugo*

As I've already said, every soul comes into this life with work to be done, a particular path it's intended to follow. And every soul is born with a particular time to go out and move on. Death, in other words, isn't the end; it's more like a stepping-stone to another level of existence.

WHEN IT'S TIME TO MOVE ON

Just as the spirits help us to come to terms with their passing and get on with the unfinished business of our own lives—which is, after all, the purpose of our being here—we can, and should, help them to let go of this life and move on when their time has come. Sometimes that's easier than other times. If a person has lived a long life or is ill and obviously suffering, it may seem natural for us, if we love that person, to let him or her know that it's okay to let go.

I always tell people that they need to say farewell and pray for the easy passing of the soul in whatever way seems natural and comfortable for them. Prayer, as I've already said, is a very personal thing, and it doesn't necessarily have to mean getting down on your knees and speaking to God. If you believe at all in the eternity of the soul, you must also believe that there's some organizing principle or higher power guiding the world of spirit, and however you conceptualize that guiding spirit, you can ask for its help to see your loved one safely across. No one ever wants a loved one to die, but you do want to help him or her with the process, which is, in any case, inevitable.

The problem with so many of us here on earth is that, too often, we want to make death be about us. If the person who's dying is someone we love very much, whom we depend on or whom we just want to be with us, we almost seem to be blaming that person for dying. "How could he do that to me?" "What am I going to do without her?" We can be very selfish when it comes to letting go of a loved one, and the soul who's ready to pass knows that. If it's really that person's time, our holding on just makes it more difficult for him or her to make the transition, which is why, as I've already mentioned, so many people pass just at the moment when their loved ones have left the room.

It may be easier to let go of a loved one once you understand that he or she will always be with you in the world of spirit.

Not too long ago I met with four sisters whose mother had died of pancreatic cancer. Near the end of her time, she was in a hospice, and her daughters visited her every day. One evening, no sooner had they left to go to dinner than she passed, and they were having a very difficult time accepting not only her passing but also the fact that they hadn't been there when she died. I explained to them that part of their mother's preparation for death was choosing her time to go. She certainly knew how much her daughters loved her and would miss her, so leaving them when they were not physically present was no doubt easier for her. They were not responsible for her choice, and they certainly had no reason to feel guilty about it.

Often, especially when people are very ill or just very old, they are able to prepare for death. They may choose to die at home or go into hospice care. They do whatever it is that will make it easier and more acceptable for them to go. And sometimes what's easier for them may not be easier for you. You just need to understand that this is what they wanted, and if you are able to do that, you'll be making it easier on yourself as well.

People often know when it's their time to
move on.

Nurses and people who work in hospice care have told me that just before someone is going to die, he or she will very often call out names or appear to be speaking with others who have already passed. Someone might say, "My mother is in the room" or "My sister was just here." I believe this means that the person is getting ready to cross over, and his or her loved ones on the other side are there to make the transition easier. In fact, one nurse told me about a patient who said to her, "I won't be here for lunch today. Give it to someone else," and, in fact, he passed that very morning.

You can help make that transition easier, too. No matter how sad you are or how much you will miss your relative or partner or even a good friend, I'm sure you want that person's soul to be at rest. Souls are able to rest when they know you're okay. But if you can't come to terms with their death and let go, even though it's their time, your dead loved one will be concerned about you, and that concern will prevent his or her soul from resting.

Sometimes, however, it's not yet time for a person to go because there's still work to be done on this plane.

KNOWING WHEN THE TIME IS RIGHT

I'm sure you've heard or read about near-death or out-of-body experiences—people who say that while they were unconscious they were traveling through a long tunnel toward "the light" but someone at the other end sent them back. Or you may have heard someone say he was floating above his own unconscious body looking down on himself in the bed.

People may have more than one time when they could go out. If they come back it's because the time was not right.

These are souls who could have gone out at that time but didn't because they realized or were told by someone in spirit that the time wasn't right. I know that I've said no one ever dies "by mistake." However and whenever you go, it is part of your soul's plan. No one else can change that, and that's why it's so senseless for anyone to beat himself or herself up about how, when, or why someone dies. It's also true, however, that each of us may have more than one moment when we *could* go, and we may not go the first time because we still need to be here.

I asked Dr. Raymond Moody, a great pioneer in the investigation of near-death experiences, whether everyone who comes close to death reports having such an encounter. He told me they didn't, but that it's difficult to know how many actually do, for the simple reason that the experience is very personal and the patient my be reluctant to discuss it.

"In one study conducted in the Netherlands," he said, "it seemed that about 20 percent of people who underwent cardiac arrest had the experience. But, on the other hand, a cardiologist I met in Denver several years ago had resuscitated about sixteen hundred people and felt that about 60 percent of them had the experience. He was a very relaxed person who conveyed concern for others, so it would be natural to assume that people might open up to him. But, clearly, there's an inherent difficulty in making that kind of assessment.

"Frankly, I don't really know why some have the experience and others don't, but we know that it doesn't have anything to do with age, gender, religious background, or the cause of their close encounter with death.

"In terms of what effect it has on people's lives, as a physician I'm not always able to follow up on what happens to my patients once they leave my care, but it seems to me that it brings them a kind of peace and that their lives are qualitatively different from those of people who do not have the experience.

"Bruce Grayson, a psychiatrist at the University of Virginia, studied people who had attempted suicide and found that some did and others didn't have near-death experiences. He then followed both groups for some time after and found that the ones who didn't have the experience continued to have a high rate of attempts at self-destruction while those who did had essentially a zero rate of subsequent attempts. When asked, those in the latter group said they'd found out from their near-death experience that life has a purpose and that there was a reason for them to be here."

I went on to ask Dr. Moody whether everyone who had a near-death experience reported that he or she had been sent back. He told me that some did, but others said they had been given a choice. "Almost invariably," he went on, "they told me they'd come back because they had young children left to raise. From their own perspective, they'd rather have stayed, but they came back for their children. Still a third group said they had no idea why they got back. One moment they were in the light and then the next moment they found themselves back in the body."

One thing that is clear is that a near-death experience can be a wake-up call that changes the direction of our life and puts us on the path we're meant to be following. That's what happened to one gentleman I met who had been leading a totally nonproductive and self-destructive life, drinking and partying to excess, when he was in a terrible car accident that catapulted him through the windshield and left him with a traumatic head injury requiring more than sixty stitches. Afterward he was told that he'd come literally within inches of being decapitated. When he finally recovered, he pulled himself together, moved out of state, started a very successful business, and has now completely reinvented himself.

Or simply having the experience of seeing what it's like for those who've crossed over may create the need to return and tell others about one's experience. Elisabeth Kübler-Ross describes the experience of one such man in her book *On Life After Death*. It seems that this person came to one of her speaking engagements to share his story with the audience of hospice workers she was addressing. As she explains in her book, he had been in a car with his entire family driving to spend the Memorial Day weekend with out-of-town relatives when the car was hit by an oil tanker, and his wife, children, and parents-in-law were all killed instantly. Only he survived, and the experience was so devastating for him that his entire life fell apart. He stopped working, started drinking heavily, and, by his own admission, was trying in every way he could to numb his pain. She goes on to say:

> His last recollection was that after two years of literally bumming around, he was lying on a dirt road at the edge of a forest, drunk and stoned as he called it, trying desperately to be reunited with his family. Not wanting to live, not even having the energy to move out of the road when he saw a big truck coming toward him and running over him.
>
> It was at this moment that he watched himself in the street, critically injured, while he observed the whole scene of the accident from a few feet above. It was at this moment that his family appeared in front of him, in a glow of light with an incredible sense of love. They had happy smiles on their faces, and simply made him aware of their presence, not communicating in any verbal way but in the form of thought transference, sharing with him the joy and happiness of their present existence.
>
> . . . He was so awed by his family's health, their beauty, their radiance and their total acceptance of this present situation, by their unconditional love. He made a vow not to touch them, not to join them, but to re-enter his physical body so that he could share with the world what he had experienced. It would be a form of redemption for his two years of trying to throw his physical life away.

Sometimes, however, a soul has to stay here because his or her presence is needed by a loved one still on this plane. Eva was one of those souls. She was just nine years old when she developed an extremely high fever and went into a coma because of an allergic reaction to medication. At the time, her parents were in the midst of an acrimonious divorce and each of them was blaming the other for what had happened to Eva. Every day her mother was at her bedside, talking to her and praying for her recovery. Thankfully, Eva survived, and when she regained consciousness she told her mother a remarkable story. She said that she'd heard conversations her parents were having that didn't take place in her hospital room and that she'd seen her mother crying in the kitchen of their home and blaming herself for having given Eva the medication that made her so sick. The little girl then told her mother, "That's what made me wake up, because my angels told me I had to come back."

When someone has a near-death experience, it
can change the lives of his loved ones as well
as his own.

In the end, Eva's near-death experience turned out to be the catalyst that turned her parents' lives around. They stayed together, stopped bickering, and resolved to make the marriage work. Eva's illness as well as her recovery were part of her own soul's purpose, and part of that purpose was to help her parents find their true paths as well.

An equally remarkable experience was recounted to me

by Beatrice. She was on the operating table undergoing a rela-
tively simple operation when her heart stopped twice. Each time
the doctors were able to resuscitate her and continue the surgery,
but when she was in the recovery room she flat-lined again and
remained in a light coma for some time. When she regained consciousness, Beatrice said that she had seen her mother, who told
her that she had to go back because, "You have two kids. There's
going to be a problem with your daughter, and you need to be
there." Sure enough, her daughter did come down with a serious
viral infection that kept her hospitalized for more than a week.
She recovered, but she needed her mother to help see her
through the crisis, and Beatrice was able to do that.

When Problems Remain Unresolved, It's Easy to Get Stuck

I don't know what would have happened to Eva's or Beatrice's
loved ones had they not come back, but I do know that they did
come back because it wasn't their time to leave. Karma plays a
role in these situations insofar as they relate to learning important lessons and completing unfinished business. Sometimes,
however, souls do pass over leaving problems or issues unresolved—their own or those of their loved ones—and even
though that, too, is part of their soul's path, it can make things a
lot more difficult for either or both of them. Remember that
souls, like the rest of us, are still working out their lessons, and
sometimes they can be confused about where they are and when
they need to let go. Those who were particularly stubborn about
learning (or not learning) while they were alive will be just as
stubborn on the other side.

If a soul crosses over without finding peace in this life, that anger or frustration or dissatisfaction will cross with her and make it difficult for her to move on. Very often, these people will have led troubled lives; they might be alcoholics or drug addicts, abusers, or simply people who were miserable for whatever reason. If they can't or won't take responsibility for their own problems, if they continue to blame others for their unhappiness, they can easily get stuck and remain earthbound instead of completing the transition. They don't want to leave, and their negative energy can make it difficult for those left behind. Sometimes people interpret their problems as being simply bad luck, but it isn't; it's the bad energy of a soul not allowing them to move on.

Troubled souls create problems for themselves
as well as their loved ones because neither of
them is able to move on.

Another reason why a soul doesn't move on may be that he is frightened of death because he hasn't made peace with his passing or is terrified of giving up control. Remember what Dr. Jane Greer said about death being the ultimate unknown and the ultimate "letting go." A soul who can't or won't let go can create a great deal of difficulty for the living. A possessive or jealous husband, for example, who can't bear the idea of someone new coming into his wife's life, may stick around to be sure that doesn't happen. She will feel that negative energy, and it can be extremely depressing and disruptive. One young woman whose husband had died was having a terrible time establishing any kind of relationship with a man because her husband was bound and determined that she wouldn't. When he came through for me, we simply had to ask him in a very polite way to move on, and once he understood the problems he was causing, he was willing to do that. Control freaks, however, don't change just because they've passed; they like to hang around and try to control us even from the other side.

Don't make it too comfortable for a troubled soul to stick around.

One way to clear the energy if you feel the presence of a lingering, disruptive spirit is to change things around in your home. Literally move the furniture. Keep a few mementos if you want, but don't leave everything just as it was. A troubled spirit is usually confused or uncomfortable with his passing, which is why he tends to hang around a place that's familiar. You certainly can—and should—honor his passing, even create some kind of shrine, if that will help you, but—for his sake as well as your own—you don't want him to feel so cozy and comfortable that he doesn't move on.

Sometimes, however, it can be the spirit who is doing the moving, as was the case for a woman whose son had died in a car accident. He had driven off the road and hit a tree, and because he had previously suffered from depression, the police had ruled his death a suicide and never really investigated any further. His mother was angry with him for having taken his own life, and virtually every day when she got home from work, she would find that a piece of furniture had mysteriously moved in her house. The whole experience was so disturbing that eventually she called upon me to help her. When I was able to make contact with the son, he let me know that in actuality another driver had cut him off and his death was accidental, not a suicide as the police were claiming. The reason my client had been experiencing so much movement of heavy objects was that her son had been trying to get her attention to let her know that. Once she knew the truth, she stopped being angry, the furniture stopped moving, and both of them were able to move on. Souls want these kinds of issues to be resolved, and if they aren't, the souls will stick around until they are.

"Forgiveness is the fragrance that the violet
sheds on the heel that has crushed it."
—*Mark Twain*

One important way to release the negative energy of a troubled soul is to let the person know you forgive her—even if she can't forgive herself or never took responsibility in the first place. You know the expression "something's got to give"? Well, it's also true that someone's got to forgive—and if the troubled soul can't do it, the ball, so to speak, is in your court. If both of you keep hanging on to your anger or resentment, you'll both get stuck.

Do yourself a favor and forgive your loved one in spirit. Staying angry is a sure way to create more problems for yourself.

A couple of years ago I met with a young woman named Maggie whose father had abandoned the family when she was eleven and her sister was thirteen. He had tried to re-enter their lives when the sisters were seventeen and nineteen, but neither of the girls would have anything to do with him. He died of a heart attack not long after, without ever having been able to remedy the mistake he'd made so many years ago.

Maggie had a history of making very bad choices in her relationships; she kept being drawn to men who were unable to commit. I explained that her father had not moved on because he'd never been able to resolve his relationship with her and that he was, therefore, affecting the choices she was making in her present relationships. Happily, I was able to help Maggie and her father complete the closure they'd never been able to achieve while he was alive. Her dad came through and made it clear to me that Maggie knew only one side of the story. He'd tried to maintain a relationship with both his daughters after leaving his marriage, but their mother had been so angry that she'd turned her daughters against him. As a result, Maggie had always longed to feel her father's love, and because she could never do that, she remained angry with him and was constantly re-creating her childhood abandonment in her adult relationships. Once she was able to see the whole picture, Maggie understood that her father really did love her, he was able to find the peace he'd been missing, and they were both able to move forward.

"Where two discourse, if the one's anger rise,
The man who lets the contest fall is wise."

—*Euripides*

Souls who get stuck can be real troublemakers, not only for their own loved ones but sometimes also for people they didn't even know, particularly for those who are troubled or vulnerable themselves. I came in contact with one of those troublemakers a few years ago, and it was a very unsettling experience.

A woman called me to meet with her nineteen-year-old daughter, Sally, a very talented artist who had gone into a deep depression. She thought I'd be able to help Sally resolve whatever problems were troubling her. When I walked in, I was greeted by a very pretty and voluptuous young woman with long brown hair who immediately said, "I put on your favorite perfume. Can you smell it?" (She was wearing musk, which was my favorite perfume at the time, but there was no way she could have known that.) Then, as she showed me into the living room, she said, "And I've also put on your favorite music." At the time, it was the Elton John song "Bennie and the Jets," and that's what was playing.

Troubled souls can make trouble for people
who are emotionally unstable.

Even though, as I'll be discussing in Chapter 5, I sometimes have premonitory dreams before meeting a new client, when Sally said those things to me, it was really kind of creepy. I think that a restless or unhappy soul, who realized that Sally's depression had made her emotionally vulnerable, took the opportunity to get to me through her. The negative spirit was able to take over her mind and, through her, try to manipulate me, frighten me, and cause me to doubt my own beliefs. I admit that the experience was extremely disconcerting, but because I was confident and mentally grounded enough to understand what was happening, I was able to let the spirit know it wasn't welcome and needed to leave the vulnerable young woman alone. Because she was depressed to begin with, her tendency was to look toward the dark side and be drawn to negative rather than positive energy. In the end, Sally's mother brought in a priest to bless the house and pray for her daughter. That helped to free her from the negative energy of the spirit, and then Sally began therapy to help her with her depression.

The best way I know to be certain that both you and the one in spirit are able to find peace is to make peace with his or her passing, however it comes about.

MURDER, ACCIDENTS, AND SUICIDE

The hardest deaths to accept are those that seem "unnatural" to us—a murder, a fatal accident, or a suicide. But if you understand what I've been saying all along—that every death is meant to be because it's part of the person's soul path—you'll be able to understand that even these unnatural deaths are part of the natural order.

That's what I explained to Patricia when she came to me distraught after her son, Michael, was killed in a gang-related shooting. She didn't understand how Michael could have become involved with a gang in the first place and she blamed herself for not having protected him. Michael, however, came through and explained that he'd joined a gang because he was scared to refuse them and didn't really know any better. It wasn't Patricia's fault. She couldn't have known because he'd never confided in her, and he hoped that she would find a way to help other young people so that they didn't have to die the same way. Once she could come to peace with his passing, that's exactly what Patricia did. She actually put her own life at risk by going out into the streets to talk to kids who were involved with gangs and help them to turn their lives around.

As I've said before, losing a loved one can be a truly life-changing experience for the one left behind and can put us on a path we'd never otherwise have traveled. When our life is turned around by an act of violence, we can be motivated to change the lives of others for the better. Patricia did that by rescuing kids from gangs; another client, whose daughter had been abused and ultimately killed by a violent husband, did it by advocating for the protection of battered women. Turning tragedy into something positive is one way to help us move on from a loss and find our true path.

Losing a loved one in an accident—particularly if it was caused by another individual—is another form of death that's tough to accept. I remember particularly a woman who was in the habit of going to the local mall with her daughter so that they could spend some "girl time" together. One day, the daughter had other plans and wasn't able to go. Her mother was killed by a drunk driver on the way to the mall, and her daughter wasn't able to forgive herself. Although I told her it wasn't in her soul's plan to be there and she couldn't have prevented what happened, she wasn't able to let go until the driver who'd caused the accident was convicted of manslaughter. That brought the closure she needed, and she was able both to honor her mother's death and find an outlet for her grief by becoming an outspoken crusader against drunk driving.

In another situation, however, the one who believed he "should have been there but wasn't" simply couldn't overcome his survivor's guilt. Tim was nineteen years old when his two best friends were killed in a car accident. The three of them had been together in the car, but they'd dropped Tim off on his corner just blocks from where the accident occurred.

Tim couldn't get over his guilt. He truly believed, even though he hadn't been driving and no matter what anyone—including his friends' families—told him, that if he'd been there he could have prevented the accident. When I met with him at his distraught mother's request, I realized that he was on an extremely self-destructive path and cautioned her that he needed to see a therapist.

People who throw their life away because they can't come to grips with someone else's passing are creating two tragedies instead of one.

Less than a year later, Tim's mother called again to give me the sad news that he had died of a drug overdose. He'd cut himself off from his family and simply thrown his life away. No one could have changed what he did—any more than he could have prevented his friends' deaths—because he was totally bent on self-destruction.

Suicide is one of the most difficult deaths for any loved one to accept because on the one hand we always think we "should have known" or could have prevented it, and on the other hand we tend to look at it as something the person who takes his or her own life has done to us. If we stop to think about it, both these reactions are just different ways of making another person's suicide be about us, but the suicide survivor is often so baffled, horrified, and frustrated that he or she simply can't see the truth—that no one can ever be responsible for anyone else's actions, whatever those actions might be.

Although there are a few instances in which a person commits suicide out of spite, because he or she is mean-spirited and in some sick way wants to get back at a family member, my personal experience with suicide is that the person is almost always so lost that he or she simply snaps, loses touch with reality, and doesn't even know what he or she is doing. When I say lost in this context I mean that the person has strayed far from his or her soul's purpose or has never been able to figure out what his or her path was meant to be. These are clearly troubled souls, and our prayers and forgiveness can help them to find peace. Most likely, however, the suicide will reincarnate very quickly because he or she has so much unfinished business to work out.

COPING WITH THE DEATH OF A CHILD

Of all the so-called unnatural deaths, the one that's most difficult for most people to accept is the death of a child—and it doesn't matter how old the child is; he or she is always our baby. One of the most rewarding aspects of my work is being able to let parents know that their child may be gone physically but is still with them, and that he or she is okay. Cynthia was devastated when her fourteen-year-old daughter, Tammy, was killed by a hit-and-run driver while crossing the street with her friends. When Cynthia came to me, she just showed me a picture of three teenagers and said, "I'd like a reading on the girl in the white shirt." I'll let her tell you about it in her own words.

CYNTHIA'S STORY

"Jeffrey was very specific about what had happened that night. He said that she was hit by a car and died instantly. The girls had been crossing at the corner when the light changed and they were caught in the middle of the street on the double line. The other girls stayed there, but Tammy got scared and ran across. That's when she was hit. The newspapers had reported that all three of them ran across and only Tammy was hit, but after the reading, I asked one of her friends, who confirmed that what Jeffrey said was true. That actually made me feel better, because I'd been wondering why, if all three girls ran into the street, my daughter was the only one hit. Jeffrey also told me that she died on impact and that they had worked on her, doing CPR, for thirty or forty minutes. At the time, I didn't know that either, but when I went back and asked the police, I found out it was, in fact, true.

"Her gravestone has two angels kneeling at the gates of heaven, and there's a photograph of Tammy between them. Jeffrey saw all that, and he told me Tammy didn't like the picture because one side of her hair was flat and the other side was wavy but that it was okay for me to keep it. When I went back and looked at the picture again, I saw that he was exactly right, and her friend Sandy agreed that Tammy wouldn't have liked that.

"There were so many details that it was absolutely amazing to me. Jeffrey knew her boyfriend's name and said that he was very troubled by her death but that there was nothing I could do to help him—all true.

"He also told me that her room was lavender—which it was—and that Tammy said it was okay for me to change it. That was amazing to me because I hadn't wanted to change it, and that had been the subject of many discussions with my husband and my friends.

"Then my mother came through and said that Tammy and I were clones—which is something she said all the time when she was alive and which, again, was true. We looked exactly alike, we had very similar body types, and we even acted alike. Jeffrey also told me that my mother had been there to greet Tammy when she crossed over.

"There were so many specifics he couldn't possibly have known that sitting there with him was like having a long-distance conversation with my daughter while Jeffrey acted as the translator. Her coming through gave me confirmation that she was still very much with me and that she's okay. I've always believed in some kind of eternal life, that there was something out there, and this whole experience was very validating."

Even as I'm writing this, I'm struck—as I'm sure you will be reading these stories—by how many children and teenagers are killed in car accidents. Another who comes to mind is Adam, who was a passenger in a car being driven by a designated driver who was, nevertheless, as Adam's mother, Candice, put it, "under the influence of marijuana" at the time. Adam was nineteen years old. He died instantly.

I didn't meet Candice and her husband, Jeff, until a year and a half later, but her seeking to know that her son was okay and still with her began shortly after he died.

"The first thing I wanted to know," Candice said, "what I think every parent wants to know, was that wherever he was, he was okay. I always knew he was somewhere. It's not that I wasn't a believer and Jeffrey turned me into a believer, it's just that I'd never had much need to go to a medium or a psychic before. I just always believed there's something more than here. But still, you don't *know*, and when it's your child you desperately have to know that he's okay and that someday you'll be together.

"My husband and I did see one other person before Jeffrey. I called her just about two weeks after Adam died. Like Jeffrey, she had appointments a long time in advance, but when we met she told me that something had just told her to pick up the phone that day. What she said was, 'Your son made me give you an appointment.'

"My husband and I saw Jeffrey twice, once about three years ago and then again around Mother's Day 2005. By the time we saw Jeffrey I was a little more settled, but I still needed to check out what I'd heard the first time and I just needed a little more validation. We walked in the door, and even before we sat down, Jeffrey turned to my husband and said, 'Oh, your father's here with a young man.' He had no idea why we were there. We'd been very careful not to give any information away. So when he said that I totally froze. In fact, I was so shocked that I forgot to turn on the tape recorder I'd been so careful to bring with me. As he talked, it was amazing how he captured their essence, their character—Adam, my father-in-law, and eventually also my mother-in-law. Of course, all I wanted to know about was Adam, but you can't control that, and whoever came through, their personalities were so vivid it was as if they were in the room with us."

Candice's husband agrees. "If someone had approached me about seeing a psychic before Adam died," he says, "I probably would have been polite and then shaken my head and mumbled, 'You're nuts!' But, as Candice said, when this happens to you, you're looking for anything to try to find comfort. For me, it wasn't so much wanting to know he was okay as just wanting to make contact and trying to communicate. I went open-minded, probably not as receptive as my wife but also not skeptical.

"What Jeffrey had to say about my parents fit them to a tee. A lot of unresolved issues between my father and me came up in that first reading, and they were absolutely on target. The second time he came through right away, too, and not just the way he came through to us but the way he related to my mother was so on target that it was as if we were sitting in their house after dinner when she was irritating him and he was egging her on. It wasn't only what they said but their personas that came through. I remember telling Candice, 'After this session they're going to have to send me into counseling.'"

The second reading, as Candice said, was just before Mother's Day about three years after the first one. This time Jeff and Candice also brought their daughter, Adam's younger sister Mariel, who was not quite seventeen when he died.

"We'd made this appointment with Jeffrey, and I just threw out to her that maybe she'd like to come with us. She'd gone with us before, but this time she was more willing and open to it. Jeffrey was speaking mostly to her—I don't even know if he remembered our first reading. But lo and behold, my father- and mother-in-law were there again, and they were arguing with each other just the way they did in life. My daughter remembered them well, and it was very real to her to have them there and also her brother. Adam was giving her advice about her boyfriend and saying all kinds of things that Jeffrey couldn't possibly have known.

Mariel describes the experience this way. "I would say I was definitely more willing to go this time. In the past, I'd gone more or less to humor my parents. But, after a previous one-on-one experience with another medium that had gone very well, I was truly looking forward to this appointment.

"When we got to Jeffrey Wands's office, I kept my mouth shut as always so as not to reveal any information. Like my father, I'm slightly apprehensive and skeptical about these sorts of things while my mother often does reading on the subject and is much more spiritual with regard to contacting my brother.

"Sure enough, my grandparents came through, but most importantly, so did Adam. Even though I was young when my grandparents died, the way Jeffrey captured their relationship and personalities, it was as though he'd invited them into the room, and that made me smile because it really brought back childhood memories.

"When he spoke about my brother, a lot of what he had to say was directed to me. Adam [through Jeffrey] talked about many aspects of my life, including college, my boyfriend, and important life decisions. It's funny, because my parents often give me advice, but hearing 'my brother's voice' through Jeffrey, I was willing to listen and to value his words.

"I guess it was the comfort and assurance I got from my experience with Jeffrey that allowed me to smile and cry during the session and then walk away with good brotherly advice as well as a much-needed contact and the knowledge that he is somewhere safe."

Candice agrees with her daughter about the value of the experience. "I think it's very healing for anybody, but especially for parents who desperately, desperately need to know that their child is with them and that eventually they'll all be together. And I also think it helped my daughter. I think it gave her just a bit of hope and lightened her a little bit. I'm very glad that she went and that Jeffrey picked up on her need to hear from her brother.

"Besides our readings with Jeffrey, one of the things that's helped my husband and me was joining Compassionate Friends, a support group for parents who've lost children. We heard about the group from several different people shortly after Adam died. At that point you're struggling to survive, you'll do anything. So we went.

"I know that at the time we were still in shock, but I was frightened to see so many people so paralyzed by their grief. My husband and I had both gone back to work a couple of weeks after Adam's death, but I now realize that we were still numb and functioning—though not very well—on autopilot. After the numbness—or the shock—wore off, it started to hit us and we understood how tough it really was.

"Compassionate Friends, in addition to giving you people to talk to who have been through the same thing you have, also provides you with all kinds of coping tools—how to get through the holidays, how to deal with people who don't want to hear about your child because it's too difficult for them. You find that you have to turn something so horrible into something that's even just a little bit positive. You have to learn how to survive and get through the rest of your life. Some people turn to religion; some people are so angry that they turn away from religion, but I think that most of them are a little bit more open than they would have been before. When something like this happens, it changes your whole belief system.

"You may know logically that there's nothing you could have done to prevent it, but, nevertheless, you're the parent and you're supposed to be the one to protect your child, so you failed. That's why a combination of bereavement counseling and whatever other support you can get is so important. You have to learn to be gentle with yourself and carry on and not beat yourself up on top of the loss."

Both Cynthia's and Candice's children died suddenly and completely unexpectedly, but even if a parent knows that his or her child will not be here long, when death actually comes it is equally devastating. Cathy's son, Justin, was diagnosed with colon cancer when he was just ten years old and, defying the doctors' prognosis, lived for six years. But, as Cathy explained, even though she knew his time was limited, when he finally passed over, she had almost been able to convince herself that it wasn't going to happen.

"Justin was a terrific kid. He was as bright as could be and couldn't have cared less. All he ever wanted to do was make people laugh. For example, for a science fair, Justin chose to grow "hair" on several different Chia Pets using a variety of substances. He also played the drums, and because of his diagnosis he had the opportunity to meet many people who became extremely close and special to him. Initially he met Johnny Depp, who took him on a movie set, took him into his trailer, let him play with his dog, and was just very good to him. Then he met the actress Mary McCormack, who turned out to be his savior. Through her he also met Howard Stern and Hank Azaria, both of whom were also extremely kind. But Mary was special. She was always there for him, no matter how busy she was, right up to the end.

"In any case, after Justin died, I couldn't believe it was actually over. A friend of mine who was a bereavement counselor told me that some of her patients had gone to a psychic—who turned out to be Jeffrey—and that he'd helped them a lot. So I figured, what did I have to lose, and I went. I didn't tell him why I was there, but almost immediately he said, 'Your son's right here,' and he described Justin to a tee. What's funny to me now is that every time Justin comes through he's wearing the clothes I buried him in, which for me throws a whole new light on how we ought to pick the clothes our loved ones are going to wear in the casket!

"I don't even remember exactly what Jeffrey told me that day, but just the fact that I knew where Justin was, I knew what he was doing, and he knew what I was doing—in other words that we could continue our relationship—made all the difference to me.

"When I got home that night, I smelled something

burning, so I looked around the house, but nothing was going on. Then I went into my room to get ready for bed, and the next thing I knew I heard a loud *pop*. I ran out to the living room and right near the door I saw a ball of burning bright white light that went through the door and dissipated. It was the most amazing thing I'd ever seen, and when I later described it to Jeffery he told me it was Justin and that putting out that kind of energy was very difficult for someone in spirit to do. He's come to me since then, mostly in dreams, but I've never had that kind of dramatic experience again.

"Now I see Jeffrey mainly on Justin's birthday. He always has some kind of validating message that helps me keep the connection. I still feel that Justin is living with me. Jeffrey has made me understand that Justin literally still knows everything that's going on in my life, and that he's doing great. Truthfully, without him I don't think I'd have made it. And for me the best part is knowing that Jeffrey also loves Justin. I don't need to see any other psychics and I don't need to share my experiences with anyone else. If other people choose not to believe, that's their choice, and it's not up to me to convince them. It's just very comforting to know that my son is with family and that he's being taken care of."

One thing I've learned in the course of my work is that children often know when they're not going to be here very long. Many grieving parents have told me, the confusion clear in their voice, that their child had told them in advance that he or she would be leaving soon.

Martha Copeland's daughter, Cathy, died in a car accident in 2001, when she was twenty years old. Martha tells her
daughter's story in her book *I'm Still Here,* and when I spoke to
her she told me that, from the time she was very young, Cathy
seemed to know she wouldn't be here long. "When she was a little girl," Martha said, "she used to tell me she was going to be
Casper the Friendly Ghost, and when I got upset with her she'd
say, 'Mom, I think it would be kind of cool to be a ghost.' When
she was six years old she cheated death for the first time. A dog
attacked her and pretty much scalped her. The doctors didn't
think she'd make it, and if she did, they said, she'd be brain damaged. She was in a coma, and when she came to she said that
she'd seen me crying and knew she had to come back to make
me happy.

"She had so many close calls before she died. If you saw
her after the dog attack, she looked like a freak, but she didn't
have any brain damage and she grew up to be a very pretty girl.
Then, just three weeks before the car accident that killed her, she
was in another accident with her cousin Rachel. The car they
were in went under an eighteen-wheeler tractor-trailer and both
girls got out without a scratch. The police and firemen who arrived on the scene were just standing there with their mouths
hanging open because they said there was no way these girls
could have escaped that kind of accident unharmed.

"After that Cathy wrote a poem that I found in her room
after she died. It wasn't addressed to me, but I knew it was meant
for me. It talked about the fact that I shouldn't miss her after she
was gone and that we'd be back together someday.

"Just a couple of days before she was killed, she came
into my room and said, 'Mom, you're going to miss me when

I'm gone,' and she started crying. She just knew she was going to go. I think that after the dog attack, because I was a single mother at the time, she knew she had to come back for me. Then, after the first car accident, she knew Rachel wouldn't be able to handle it if she died and that it would tear the family apart. She had to go when it was the right time."

Since her death, Cathy has been contacting Martha through Electronic Voice Phenomena (EVP). "The first time Cathy's voice came through, it was to Rachel," Martha said. "After the first accident, they'd made a pact that if one of them should die, the one in the spiritual world would come back and let the one in the physical world know she was okay. Cathy was teasing Rachel, saying, 'I'm going to come back and write Cat, Cat, Cat, all over your computer screen. One night about five months after she died, Rachel couldn't sleep, so she got up and turned on her computer. She was online when she saw something about EVP, so she started trying to do it. She'd been at it for hours when she got really frustrated and started kicking things around her room and crying, saying, 'Cat, you promised you'd come back and now you've left me. I'm all alone.' Then she sat down and tried one more time, and when she played it back she heard Cathy's voice saying, 'I'm still here,' and then a male voice saying, 'How do you know they can hear you?' And then a big sigh from Cathy. Rachel called me the next day and told me I had to come over. She had Cathy's voice on her computer. My husband and I were so excited that we actually got lost driving to my sister's house. After I heard it I was in shock for two days. I always knew there was something on the other side, but just to have that voice come back again and know that she was happy . . . I immediately started trying it myself, just using my computer the way Rachel had.

"I didn't even know what EVP was at the time, but gradually I started doing some research and started using more sophisticated recording equipment. Now I have recorders all over the house. One incident I'll never forget occurred when I was in the kitchen snapping green beans for Thanksgiving. My sister called and asked if I wanted to go shopping with her, so I left the bowl of snapped beans on the kitchen table and left. When I got back, Cathy's dog, Doja, had gotten into the beans and spit them out all over the room. It was a total mess, and when I played back the recorder that had been on in the kitchen, I heard Cathy's voice saying, 'Doja, no!'

"At first, after she died, I thought, 'What a waste of a life.' She was just twenty years old and getting ready to move out of the house and live on her own for the first time. But now I realize that there was a reason for her death. It's helped a lot of other parents through their grief."

After Martha's initial experiences, she formed the Recording Circle—Bridge to the Afterlife, a group of parents who get together to use EVP to contact their loved ones in spirit, and she is now on the board of the American Association of Electronic Voice Phenomena.

For those of you who are unfamiliar with EVP, it is, to me, very much like what I do when I "hear" what souls are communicating to me by tuning in to their energy. Because not everyone is able to do that as easily as I am, and because those in spirit are composed of pure energy, they look for an electronic means of making their messages more accessible to their loved ones—electricity, after all, is itself a form of pure energy. I myself have taken a simple digital recorder into a cemetery and received EVP messages from souls who were lingering there. In Chapter 6 I'll be talking more about why some souls do not move on but continue to linger near the place where their body was buried. In terms of EVP, however, it is a way for them to make their spiritual vibrations from another dimension audible to us on this plane. I've also found that when clients tape their sessions with me and later play back the tape, there may be EVPs on the recording along with our own voices. In those instances, the audible message is almost always from a loved one who has come through to me during the reading.

In Martha's case, Cat's having discussed her death beforehand primed her mother to accept the existence of a different kind of consciousness, and her messages, delivered by means of EVP, are her way of reassuring Martha of the existence of life after death.

I met Martha and Karen Mossey, her partner in the Recording Circle, when Maury Povich produced a show to tie in to the movie *White Noise*. I had no idea who they were at the time, but as I sat down to talk to them I was able to bring Cathy through, along with Martha's father. I then learned that these two women had been brought together by their children on the other side, a remarkable case of souls putting people in our path that Martha discusses in her book.

Martha's story is unique in the sense that it encompasses so many aspects of the spiritual realm: her daughter's knowing from an early age that she would die young, her near-death experience after the dog attack, and the apparent intervention that saved her and her cousin from going out in the first car accident. But many other children seem to have the same kind of prescience regarding their own death.

Because children are more open to what comes
at them from the world of spirit, they can
often sense when they are going to pass on.

A mother whose seven-year-old son had been hit by a car and died, told me that he had always been deathly afraid of cars and had told her over and over that he was going to be hit by a car. She, not unnaturally, had tried to assure him that no such thing would happen, and, of course, when he did die exactly as he'd told her he would, she felt terrible that she hadn't taken his fear more seriously. When she came to see me, I explained that her son, in his soul, knew what lay in his path. She couldn't have known that, and there was certainly nothing she could have done to change or prevent it.

One reason I think that children can be so attuned to their own passing is that they're more open and in touch with their soul consciousness than adults, who are more likely to dismiss or block out their feelings or premonitions because they just don't want to know. It's the same kind of openness that allows children not only to see or receive dream visits from people in spirit but also to communicate what they've experienced without filtering it or explaining it away. It's not unusual, in my experience, for children to be able to describe and talk about relatives who died before they were born. They don't rationalize the way adults do; they just accept without question what comes to them.

For our part, we need to understand that children come into our lives just as soul mates or cellmates do, because they have something to teach us or to help us work out, or because they're working out issues from a past life of their own. Children may also be more aware than we are of having been here before and of when it's their time to pass on. A dramatic example of this was described to me by the father of a twelve-year-old boy who had told him, "Daddy, it's not my time here. I was here one other time, and it wasn't like it is now. I'm so unhappy here. I just don't fit in." Three days later, he threw himself in front of a car. In this instance the boy's mother had suffered a miscarriage before he was born, and I believe that he always felt guilty about his own birth and never believed he was "good enough" to make up for her loss. Whatever purpose he was intended to fulfill in this life, he was never able to find his way. He was never able to find peace, and so he went out of his own choosing.

Souls can sometimes come in at the wrong time or in the wrong body because they have something to work out for themselves or because they have a lesson to teach their family. I believe this is particularly true of children who are handicapped or whose birth is in some way traumatic. These children are so special that they always have a profound effect on those around them. And because all souls continue to reincarnate, they will also come back.

I encountered one fascinating example of this continual renewal of the tree of life when I met a woman who had been carrying a tremendous amount of unnecessary guilt because her mother had given birth to a stillborn son before she herself was born. Now the woman was expecting a child of her own, and her doctors were telling her that it was going to be a girl. When I sat with her, however, her grandmother came through and let me know that the baby was going to be the reincarnated soul of her stillborn brother. And sure enough, she gave birth to a boy who was, in fact, the spitting image of her own father—which is assumedly what her stillborn brother would have grown to look like if he'd lived.

Children come into our lives for a reason, and
sometimes—like other people—they also
leave us when their purpose is fulfilled.

Although I certainly understand how devastating it is to lose a child, I hope it will help parents to accept their loss if they know the death was meant to be and that it is part of their own path as well as the child's. Parents also need to understand that losing their child is not a retribution being meted out to them by a punishing god for some kind of bad behavior, even though that's what it may seem like at the time. No one is ever "taken" from us as punishment. Once again, that's a way we have of making death be all about us. In fact, nothing that happens to us in our life is ever a punishment. It may be a wake-up call, a lesson, or a way of guiding us in a new direction, but it's always to help us find our true soul purpose. And it's always up to us to "get with the program" or not.

FINDING PEACE AND MOVING ON

Just as we have to make peace with the death of a loved one in order to get on with our lives, those in spirit also need to complete their work in order to move on.

Sometimes they can do that from the other side by helping us while we're still in this life, and I've given you many examples of ways that communicating with a loved one who's crossed can do that. And sometimes they will need to come back in order to work out issues that are still unresolved on this plane. But spirits who have found their true path and completed their work evolve to a higher level and achieve eternal rest.

Once they've resolved all their issues here on earth, those in spirit stop reincarnating and move on to a higher plane.

When that happens, the one in spirit will continue to be involved in our life, but he or she will likely play the role of guardian angel or spirit guide. For most of us, that final evolution takes hundreds and hundreds of years and generally depends upon how much we have been able to do for others while we were alive. So someone like Mother Teresa, whose life was about selfless giving, may move up very quickly. Helping others is what life is supposed to be about. If we do it right, we'll be finding our own fulfillment at the same time we help others to discover their own—and doing that is the surest way we have of getting our "ticket to heaven."

SOUL PRINTS

❋ Energy never dies; it just keeps changing forms.

❋ Death isn't the end—it's a stepping-stone.

❋ When your loved one dies, it's not about you.

❋ It's our job to help our loved ones move on when their time comes.

❋ Whenever you go out, it's part of your soul's path.

❋ The hardest deaths to accept are those that seem "unnatural" to us—accident, murder, suicide, or the death of a child—but all those deaths are also part of the soul's plan.

❋ Each of us may have more than one moment when we could go.

❋ A near-death experience can be a wake-up call that changes the direction of your life.

❋ When a soul crosses over without finding peace in this life, it can be difficult for him or her to move on.

❋ Stuck souls can be real troublemakers for those left behind.

❋ Once a soul has found his true path and completed his work on this plane, he will evolve to a higher level.

4

Animals Also Have Souls

Often, people who've lost a pet are just as excited and moved to know that their pet has come through as they are to hear from a human loved one in spirit. That's how strong the bond between people and pets can be. Just because pets can't talk doesn't mean that they don't have feelings and that they aren't connected to us. And, yes, animals do have souls, and they do come back to us. In fact, they watch over us, protect us, and continue to be present in our lives in much the same way the spirits of our human loved ones do. I can personally attest to their protective instincts because once, when I was called in to investigate the presence of spirits in an old house, I was actually scratched by a cat in the world of spirit. It hurt, and the scratches were very real and very visible. The only way I can account for what happened is that the cat must have died in the house and was now protecting its turf.

If you remember that all life is energy, it shouldn't be difficult to understand that the life force or energy of the animal continues in spirit just like human energy does. In fact, in the course of my work I've come to understand that—both here and in the world of spirit—animals are very much like children. I've already talked about the fact that children tend to be more open than adults to their psychic selves. And, like children, animals often know when they're going to cross over, which is why, I think, we hear so many stories about animals who just stop eating or who go out into a field to die. Children seem highly attuned to the things that come to them from the spirit world in general, and animals are very much the same.

In fact, traditional Native American culture looks upon animals as spirit guides and considers them sacred beings blessed with spiritual energy. According to their traditional belief system, there are four distinct types of animal spirit guides that come through in dreams, signs, or symbolic events for a particular purpose. Messenger guides come into your life and stay only until the message is understood; shadow guides come to teach a lesson you haven't yet learned from repeated mistakes; journey guides appear when you come to a crossroads in your life to help you determine which path to follow; life guides remain with you for life. I believe it is impossible not to see the obvious parallels between the ways these animal spirits are believed to function in people's lives and the way human spirits function in the lives of their loved ones.

"I believe cats to be spirits come to earth."

—*Jules Verne*

Native Americans also believe that at some point in the distant past man was able to communicate directly with animals and that animals still communicate with one another telepathically. I, too, have found that animals are highly telepathic, and I don't believe that we have entirely lost our ability to communicate with them on that level. If you focus and concentrate on a particular image, you can transfer that image to the animal. I've seen this happen with my own dog, Cleopatra (affectionately known as Cleo), who, sadly, passed away just as I was finishing this book. When I used to concentrate on something like seeing Cleo lying down in her corner of the living room, almost immediately, she would go to the corner and lie down. In fact, truly gifted animal psychics will tell you that the animals put pictures in the psychic's mind so that they can "see" what the animal is "thinking."

If you have a pet, you can practice doing this. Think "leash" or "food" and see how quickly your pet goes over to the place where you keep his leash or his food. People are always telling me that their dog "knows" when they're going on a trip, and I believe that's absolutely true, because if you're going away you have pictures in your brain of packing or going to the airport, or whatever, and your dog picks up on those mental images.

"I think I could turn and live with animals,
    they are so placid and self-contained,
I stand and look at them long and long.
They do not sweat and whine about their con-
    dition,
They do not lie awake in the dark and weep
    for their sins,
They do not make me sick discussing their
    duty to God,

Not one is dissatisfied, not one is demented
   with the mania of owning things,
Not one kneels to another, nor to his kind
   that lived thousands of years ago,
Not one is respectable or unhappy over the
   whole earth."

—*Walt Whitman, "Song of Myself"*

Rupert Sheldrake, an English scientist, philosopher, and author of the book *Dogs That Know When Their Owners Are Coming Home: And Other Unexplained Powers of Animals*, has gathered a significant number of case histories documenting animals' telepathic, premonitory, and other unexplained abilities. In doing so, he has attempted to explain them in relation to his own theory of "morphic fields," which he describes as self-organizing regions of influence that interconnect and organize a system and act as "channels of telepathic communication." Frankly, I don't know anything about morphic fields, but what Sheldrake describes sounds to me a lot like energy fields, and what I do know is that animals are more sensitive to the energy that is coming at them all the time than most people I've met. (As an aside here, I recently saw a news report on television describing an experiment in which dogs seemed to be particularly accurate about literally sniffing out cancerous tumors. Without seeming too far out, I'd like to suggest that since cancer cells are living organisms, they are composed of energy, and it might just be possible that dogs are sensitive to the particular energy they give off.)

Sheldrake, like Gary Schwartz in *The Afterlife Experiments*, appears to be trying to provide scientific proof for something that, to my mind, can't be proved in terms of the knowledge we have now. I can, however, agree wholeheartedly with a question he asks in the introduction to his book: "Pets are the animals we know best, but their most surprising and intriguing behavior is treated as of no real interest. Why should that be so?"

ANIMALS CAN "SEE" WHAT MOST PEOPLE DON'T

Cleo, my golden retriever, not only "saw" the images I projected to her but also, more often than not, when I was alone in the house and became aware of a spirit being present in the room (which is something I experience quite regularly), Cleo, who was usually lying at my feet, would be aware of it, too. What generally happened was that I would become aware of a presence in the room—sometimes I just feel it, sometimes I see lights, sometimes there's a distinctive smell, sometimes it's a combination of the three—and when those phenomena occurred, Cleo instantly became alert, lifted her head, and looked around in a way that let me know she, too, felt the spirit's presence.

Cleo didn't seem to be frightened by what was happening, but that wasn't the case for my client Stacy's cat, Blackie. Stacy had bought a 1930s brownstone in Manhattan and was slowly renovating it one floor at a time. It seemed, however, that Blackie didn't want to have anything to do with the apartment across the hall from the one in which Stacy was living. In fact, every time he ventured into the hall, his back arched, his hair stood on end, and he began to hiss. Since this was far from his normally laid-back behavior, Stacy decided to do some research on the building. She found out that many years before, a tenant had hanged himself in the very apartment that Blackie seemed to be so afraid of. Stacy's interpretation—with which I agree—is that his spirit was still there. Blackie could see him even though Stacy couldn't, and he clearly didn't like what he was seeing.

Sometimes an animal's "psychicness" can be pretty funny—so long as you are able to see the humor it in. For example, a client of mine has a cat. Her father, who has passed, always hated her cat (I don't know why—sometimes people just don't like cats). Now, she says, she can be sitting in the living room alone when the cat suddenly looks at the chair where her father used to sit and races across the floor as if he were chasing something. I guess the cat was happy to be rid of his nemesis and is making his feelings known whenever her dad's spirit comes back for a visit.

IF YOUR PET IS ACTING WEIRD, PAY ATTENTION

One aspect of animals' heightened psychic awareness is their ability to sense danger. There are various explanations for animals' strange behavior just before a severe change in weather or a natural disaster. Birds gather in trees or fly away before a storm. Cats hide in closets. Dogs howl or crawl under the bed. We're told that when that happens they're reacting to a change in barometric pressure, and that may certainly be true. But, as I've discussed, animals also have an uncanny awareness of impending danger.

If your animal is acting fearful, he or she may
have good reason to be afraid.

Just before the tsunami disaster of 2004, animals fled inland to safety while the horrific tidal wave caught hundreds of thousands of people by surprise.

In fact, one of my friends, who lives in Northern California, told me that before the last major earthquake her own dog "went crazy," banging himself against the door to try to get her attention and get both of them out of the house.

In another case of a pet sensing danger, a client told me about how her dog—a Labrador retriever ironically named Lucky—had awakened the entire family in the middle of the night and literally saved them from an electrical fire in their house. Because Lucky was so rambunctious, the family at first thought he'd just chosen a particularly inappropriate time to want to play. But then they smelled the acrid smoke and realized that in this instance man's best friend was also acting as their guardian angel.

And finally there was a client's dog who saved her two-year-old son, Jason, from potentially drowning in the family's backyard swimming pool. Although the pool area was fenced, one day the gate was apparently left unlatched and the toddler wandered in. The next thing Jason's mother knew, their German shepherd was going nuts, barking his head off. When she rushed outside, she saw that the dog had actually jumped the fence and was herding Jason away from the edge of the pool.

I realize this sounds a lot like the old story of Lassie warning the family that "Timmy's in the well," and I also realize that dogs are known to be very protective of children. However, in this instance, no one was attacking Jason. He wasn't even in the pool. How did the dog know he was in danger? I believe that he was simply tuned in to a higher level of psychic consciousness.

WITH PETS, IT'S ALL ABOUT LOVE

If your pet is letting you know through his or her behavior that something is wrong, he or she is probably trying to protect you because your pet loves you. I'm sure you've heard people say, "No one will ever love me the way my dog does," and to a large degree that's absolutely true. Although the love between people can be tremendously deep and strong, it's rarely so completely nonjudgmental and unconditional as the love of a pet.

One of the most touching demonstrations of that love was told to me by a client with regard to her son, Chad, and his black Lab, Rocky. Chad was very sick with childhood diabetes and he and Rocky were inseparable—except when Rocky was displaying typical Lab behavior and "escaping" from the house or yard to chase cars or animals. One day Rocky escaped and got hit by a car. He was killed instantly and Chad was inconsolable. His mother told me that after Rocky died, he began to make regular nighttime visits, and when she looked in on Chad during the night she could clearly see the indentation made by Rocky's body sleeping next to him, just as they'd always slept when Rocky was alive.

The bond of love with your animal continues
in spirit just like the bond of love
between people.

Animals, as I've said, are not only deeply connected to us but also deeply intuitive, as was demonstrated by Sam, a Jack

Russell terrier, who was extremely close to his young mistress, Hailey, who was suffering from severe juvenile rheumatoid arthritis. It seems that just a few minutes before Hailey was about to experience a flare-up of the disease, Sam would regularly go over to her and put his head in her lap. Even in the middle of the night, he would wake up and go into her room whenever she was about to have an attack. By the time Hailey was eighteen and going off to college, Sam was also older and finally died. One day Hailey took a picture of her dorm room to send to her mother, and when the film was developed, there was an image of Sam on her bed, showing up as a bright white spot with just his paws visible.

In a kind of reverse situation, I remember a woman whose husband had died of cancer. While he was sick, he and the family dog, Franklin, had been together constantly. Then, three months after he died, Franklin died, too. Their bond had been so strong that he wanted to be with his master, and, as I told my client, her husband had come back to help him cross.

In fact, animals do rejoin their families in spirit and very often come through with them during my readings. In one particularly touching instance, a woman had lost a son to leukemia, and when he came through he was with her first dog, a terrier named Cujo, who had passed before he was born. Her son let her know that Cujo had helped him to cross over and made sure that he was okay.

COMMUNICATING WITH ANIMALS IN SPIRIT

When we think about pets, we generally assume they are dogs or cats, but there are all kinds of companion animals, and after they pass they're all out there, still bound to us in spirit. Probably the most unusual animal spirit I've encountered was that of a pet duck a woman had had when she was a little girl. I've also connected with a horse. My client used to ride her horse practically every day, and when he became ill she had to put him down. She'd been carrying an enormous amount of guilt about that decision, but when the horse came through he was able to let her know that she'd done the right thing and didn't need to feel guilty about it.

When animals in spirit communicate, there's no hidden agenda. They just love us and want to alleviate our grief.

Putting an animal down when he or she is suffering is a gift we have to give, but it's also a source of tremendous guilt for a lot of people. So when an animal comes through to let you know you made a good decision, he or she is really giving you a gift in return. The grieving process is just as complex and important when we're grieving the loss of an animal companion as when we grieve a relative or beloved friend, and when that grieving is further complicated by having chosen to help the animal pass, it can be extremely painful. I believe animals know this, and because their love is so pure and unconditional, they will do what they can to alleviate our pain.

I, as I've said, have recently gone through the very personal and deeply felt loss of my own dog, Cleo. I have to admit that I would never have guessed how much her death would affect me, but it was one of the most painful losses I've ever experienced.

Cleo had a tumor on her liver, and her vet advised us that it needed to be removed. I was extremely ambivalent about putting her through the surgery, but, in the end, my wife convinced me that we needed to do whatever we could to try to save or prolong her life. I knew, on a higher level, that she was going to die, but on a very human level, I was trying to deny what I knew because I simply wasn't ready for it to happen. She got through the surgery and, after staying in the hospital for six days, she came home. That night, we all went to bed, and at about four o'clock in the morning, Cleo woke me up to let her out. When she came back, she was panting heavily and obviously in pain. I stayed up with her through the night, trying to comfort her, telling her I loved her, and letting her know it was okay for her to go.

The next morning, as soon as our younger son left for school, Cleo went into the guest bedroom, lay down on a jacket of mine that was in there, and passed away. We'd had Cleo since our younger boy was ten months old, and I realized that she'd been waiting for him to leave—just as people often wait for their loved ones to leave the room before they pass. She picked her own time and her own way to go.

In the week following her death, every member of my family received a message from her. My wife, Dawn, had a dream in which Cleo came through with two of the dogs she'd had as a child. In the dream, Cleo came up to my wife and let Dawn pet her. My own dream was actually somewhat amusing. When Dawn was growing up, she had a pony named Coco, who was very nasty and used to bite people. In my dream, Dawn's grandfather came to tell me how glad he was to have Cleo there because she was chasing the pony and preventing Coco from biting him. Both our sons have also had dream visits from her, and we've all seen her in the house on more than one occasion. Once, when I was standing in my bedroom in my shorts, I could feel her rubbing up against me. All of us know that she's okay now, and she's still with us.

HOW ANIMALS COMMUNICATE

Animal communications are generally very simple. They usually give visual signs that they know will be meaningful to their human companions. One woman, for example, had lost her golden retriever. Because she lived near the ocean, she'd been in the habit of going to the beach with the dog every day. That was their time together and also a time for her to think through whatever was bothering her or going on in her life.

She also took the dog with her whenever she traveled, and when I did a reading for her, the dog came through with her Aunt Milly and gave me visual images of the places they'd visited together and things they'd done that were extremely specific, personal, and meaningful to her.

In yet another instance, a woman's father who had been an avid hunter came through with his pointer, Sam. He and his dog had been inseparable. Sam went to work with him, rode with him in the front seat of his car, and generally shared every aspect of his life. During my reading, he and Sam showed me visual images of all these things that let the woman know her father and his dog were still together and still bonded on the other side.

With animals, as with people, communication goes both ways, as one of my cat-loving clients discovered when she adopted the cat that had belonged to her deceased neighbor across the hall. Every night at 1 a.m., the time when his owner passed, the normally quiet cat would begin to howl and cry. I explained to her that this was the time when his former master's spirit came through and they were able to communicate with one another.

WHEN ANIMALS COME BACK TO US

Some of us are "animal people" and some of us aren't. I'm definitely an animal person, but even if I weren't, it would have become clear to me from my work how closely bonded people are with their pets.

It's because of that bond that our pets come back to us. People, as I've said, reincarnate because they still have lessons to learn about their soul's purpose. Animals, however, come back simply because they're connected to us through unconditional love and just want to be with us. For that reason they come back much more quickly, and it isn't unusual for us to get the same pet back three or four times in our own lifetime. Many of my clients have had animals reincarnate and return to them, whereas, as I said earlier, it takes a human soul at least eighty to one hundred years learning lessons in the spirit world before he or she is ready to come back. That doesn't mean every pet you have after the death of an animal will be that animal reincarnated, but when it is the same one, you will know it because the animal will show you, through actions or mannerisms, that you have been together before.

Animals reincarnate more quickly than people to be with us, not because they have any particular lesson to learn.

Moira, who used to work at my veterinarian's office, was involved in rescuing rottweilers. (For every breed there are rescue organizations composed of people who take in or find homes for abused or abandoned dogs.) She'd already had several rescued rotties and had lost one named Spike about a year and a half earlier to leukemia when someone came in, dropped off a rottweiler at the vet, and never returned. On the spur of the moment, Moira decided to adopt the dog and name him Rufus. The minute she took him home, Rufus went directly to the sofa and pulled Spike's red ball out from underneath, where it had been since he died. Then he went up the stairs with the ball and lay down on Spike's pillow.

Later on, Moira took Rufus for a ride in her car, stopping at the gas station where Spike had always barked furiously at the attendant. By that time she wasn't even surprised when her new adoptee barked furiously at the same guy. It was clear to her that Spike had come back.

In this case Spike did reincarnate as a rottweiler (maybe because Moira was so involved in rottie rescue), but animals don't always come back as the same breed. In fact, dogs sometimes return as cats, and vice versa. So if you become obsessed with "finding" your pet or expecting it to return looking exactly the same as the one who passed, you can create a great deal of unnecessary heartache for yourself. That's exactly what happened to Esther, who had lost her beloved red poodle named Red.

Esther was heartbroken after Red died and desperate to get him back. She had already consulted another psychic when she finally came to see me, and I was able to communicate with her grandmother, who let Esther know that Red would, in fact, be returning as a "reddish" poodle.

But even when Red did come back to her, Esther had a hard time believing it was really him. I had to explain to her over and over that it was Red's soul reincarnating, but that he was in a different body and, therefore, she shouldn't expect all his habits and mannerisms to be exactly the same. In the end, she finally came to understand and accept what I had been telling her—but it took her a long time.

ESTHER'S STORY

"Red had been my whole world. He was a sickly dog, and before he died he developed diabetes, kidney trouble, and problems with his pancreas. As a result, my whole world revolved around taking care of him, and he let me do whatever was necessary, including giving him insulin shots. When he passed on June 3, 2002, it was absolutely the worst thing that had ever happened in my life.

"A woman I knew suggested I go to a psychic, who told me that Red would be coming back as a small dog, a female, two-toned. Lighter in the front, darker in the back. However, she also told me there was a certain pet store on Long Island I should go to, and that Red would come to me there. Even though I don't usually talk about these things, something made me tell this story to my physical therapist, who said, 'I don't know. It seems odd to me that a psychic would tell you to go to a particular pet store.' And she told me that her husband's cousin went to a psychic he really liked—who turned out to be Jeffrey.

"So I went to Jeffrey, which was the beginning of one of the best relationships of my entire life! He, too, told me that Red would come back as a female, lighter in the front and darker in the back. And he said she would come through word of mouth. Then he also told me it would be a poodle, and my response was that this wasn't possible, since there were no two-toned poodles. But Jeffrey just said, 'Trust me!'

"At that point, I started making phone calls. I called the AKC, who gave me the number of the Poodle Club where I got the numbers of a few breeders. I gave Jeffrey the names of the breeders, and he said, 'That one. She's coming through that breeder.'

"By that time it was October. I went to see the breeder, met the dogs she'd be breeding—two females whom she'd be mating with her champion male. I left a deposit, but I still had an enormous amount of grief, and Jeffrey told me that Red wouldn't come back until I'd gotten over my grief and my relationship with him was different.

"I got through the winter, and in March I went to the Quest Bookstore and did a group meditation during which I asked when Red was coming back. The answer I got loud and clear was July. Then, that very afternoon, the breeder with whom I'd left the deposit called to tell me she was expecting a litter in May and the puppies would be ready to go in July. But in May her dog had an all-boy litter, and Jeffrey had told me that Red would come back as a girl. Now it would again be months before another litter was born.

"At that point, I went to Jeffrey and said, 'I've been good, I've had faith, but I can't stand it anymore.' Now Jeffrey told me that Red would come back as a boy. Although I was skeptical at first, he explained that sometimes a female soul will come back in a male body. Initially, he had thought Red would come back as a female because the spirits were showing him a female soul, but, as it turned out, in this instance the female soul would be returning in a male body. He also told me that Red was evolved enough that he didn't have to come back at all, and if he did it would be because of his love for me. He said it was up to me to be able to finish with my grief and get to a different place. On the anniversary of Red's death I held a private memorial ceremony, and after that I was able to let go.

"Jeffrey kept telling me that things were looking good, but he had also told me that when Red came back it would be in a litter of four—three together and one separate—and the way I would know the right puppy was that he would come to me. In June I went to pick a puppy from the breeder's new litter, but there were only three. When I saw them, I felt absolutely nothing. 'You know,' the breeder said, 'I've got another litter, and there's a female puppy I know you'll just love.'

"I couldn't tell her I wasn't interested in a female because my psychic had told me my dog would be coming back as a male. She'd think I was insane. So I went to look at the other puppies. There were three males together and a female in a separate crate. One of the males had a little white beard. He came right up to me as if to say, 'Here I am.' I put him back and went to look at the others. He came up to me again.

"By the end of the day I'd fallen in love with that little male puppy with the white beard, whom I subsequently named Winston. I took pictures of the whole litter, and when I showed them to Jeffrey, he immediately pointed to Winston and said, 'That's the one.' The white beard, of course, makes him two-tone—lighter in the front and darker in the back—just as Jeffrey had said.

"In the beginning I still had problems accepting Winston as Red because he was so active and rambunctious while Red, because he had been sickly, had always been much quieter and calmer. I would get angry at Winston and accuse him of not being Red, but Jeffrey helped me to understand that because this was a different body, the dog's personality would be different. He also told me that if I needed further proof this was Red, I just needed to realize that Red, who had been coming through with my grandmother, was no longer there because his soul was now in Winston's body.

"Eventually I was able to accept that, and now I know that my Red really has come back. Winston and I are inseparable and there is a tremendous love between us."

WE CAN LEARN A LOT FROM OUR PETS

To be loved—that's all our animals want. They'll do virtually anything for us so long as we love them, and because of that they can teach us a lot about what it means to love and be loved.

Because they love us so unconditionally and are so intuitive, animals sense what we're feeling almost before we're aware of it ourselves, and when they look at us with that wise and penetrating gaze, they're trying to communicate their compassion and concern.

Sometimes it's hard for us to love one another unconditionally, but we can take a lesson from our animal companions and try to be as giving and forgiving in our human relationships as they are of us.

———

SOUL PRINTS

❋ Animals, like children, are more open to the world of spirit than most adults.

❋ Animals have an uncanny "psychic" ability to sense danger.

❋ Our animals' love for us is unconditional and nonjudgmental.

❋ Animals in spirit are usually with family members who have also passed.

❋ Grieving for a beloved animal is as profound and complex as grieving for a human loved one.

❋ Animal communications are very simple, usually visual, and always meaningful to their human companion.

❋ Animals do come back to us.

❋ Animals reincarnate more quickly than people because they don't carry the kind of emotional baggage humans do and they just want to be with us.

❋ Animals don't always come back as the same breed or even the same species, so don't expect them to be exactly like the animal you lost. Remember—the soul is the same but the body is different.

❋ We can learn a lot about love from our pets.

5

Psychological Dreams, Psychic Dreams, and Dream Visits

People often ask me if every dream they have about someone who's passed means that person is paying them a visit. I don't believe that's true, but I do believe that virtually every dream we have has some kind of psychic significance.

Even if we're just dreaming about something that's actually happening in our life—for example, a stressful situation at work or a difficult relationship—and we know exactly where that dream is coming from, it's always a good idea to pay attention to what's happening in the dream because it may be giving us a clue about how to handle the problem. On a rational level, we may be afraid or confused, but on the dream level, we may be getting the answers we need.

Dreams can also be premonitions of things to come. When we have a premonitory dream and then repeat the experience in real life, we will probably have a strong sensation of déjà vu, the uncanny feeling that we've "been there, done that" before.

Sometimes, however, premonitions can fool us, or we fail to see the dream for what it really is—and when we do, it can be very funny. I can be fooled as easily as the next guy, and that's just what happened when I started dreaming that I was talking to Abraham Lincoln. I couldn't see his face, but I could hear his voice, and he kept quoting his most famous lines from the Gettysburg Address so that I'd be sure to know who he was. Not too long afterward, it was Presidents Day, and I was in Manhattan. I was walking up Broadway when there, right in front of me, was a guy dressed up as Lincoln advertising the opening of an electronics store. I'd thought my dream had great significance when all it turned out to mean was that I'd be seeing a guy hawking televisions on the street.

PSYCHOLOGICAL DREAMS—WHAT FREUD DIDN'T TELL US

Sigmund Freud's seminal work *The Interpretation of Dreams* tells us that dreams are our way of bringing up psychological issues that exist below the level of consciousness or that we have suppressed because they are too difficult or painful for us to deal with.

"The interpretation of dreams is the royal road to a knowledge of the unconscious activities of the mind."

—*Sigmund Freud*

While I agree that dreams are a way for us to process a lot of the issues we haven't been able to resolve in the course of our waking lives, I would add that these so-called psychological dreams also have a psychic component.

Dreams can help us to resolve issues we may
be confused about in our rational,
waking state.

One particularly significant example of this occurs when a dream provides us with an insight into a childhood or past-life experience. Lisa was a young woman who had no memory of her childhood before the age of five and who, as a child, had dreamed recurrently of being in another family and having a little brother. During our reading, her mother came through, crying and apologizing that she had never told Lisa she was adopted. Lisa's dreams were clearly a reflection of her subconscious memory of her biological family.

After our session, she was able to approach her mother's sister, who confirmed what her mother in spirit had said, and, after that, Lisa was actually able to reconnect with her birth mother and meet the younger brother she hadn't remembered at all—except in her dream

But, as I've said, dreams can go back even further than childhood to bring up issues remaining from past lives. This was the case for a woman who was pathologically afraid of water. As far as she was aware, there was no rational reason for her fear. In a dream, however, she saw herself on a ship coming to America from Europe. The ship hit a rock, she was thrown overboard, and she saw herself caught underneath the ship, unable to get to the surface and drowning. She saw all this in great detail, and when we discussed it, I was able to make her understand that her dream represented an experience she must have had in a past life.

Now she had an explanation for her fear, which gave her a starting place to work with a therapist to overcome it.

However, because dreams are often symbolic and, therefore, not always entirely clear, the insights we receive in them can also be confusing and can sometimes lead to our jumping to the wrong conclusion. Sharon, for example, was dreaming repeatedly of being touched improperly as a child, but she could never see the face of the person molesting her. In her own mind, she concluded that the molester must have been her father, who had since passed away. When she came to see me, however, her father came through and let me know that it had actually been his brother who had molested her and that he, in turn, had been molested by his own father. Sharon had obviously repressed this childhood memory because she was unable to deal with it. Once she knew the truth, she was able to get the therapy she needed to resolve her past trauma, and her nightmares stopped.

But there are other ways as well for our dreams to help us gain insight into our lives and perhaps change them for the better. Once you understand that every soul has a purpose or a path it's intended to follow, and that it can take a lot of us stubborn souls a long time to figure out what our path is supposed to be, you can see that our dreams may contain messages from our higher psychic self telling us to, in effect, wake up and smell the coffee.

These dreams can be good or bad. Let's say you dream of being in a situation or doing something you'd never consciously imagined, and in the dream you're feeling extremely happy and content. Well, maybe your psychic self is letting you know that this is something you ought to consider bringing into your life.

That "something" can even be a person. A woman came to me because she'd been dreaming of the man she was going to marry, and none of the men she was meeting seemed to be the "right" guy. The "man of her dreams" had a distinctive birthmark on his right hip, and the guy she was dating, whose name was Matt, seemed to be "the one" in every way, except that he didn't have a birthmark. Because of that one flaw, she kept rejecting him—until, in a dream, Matt's twin brother, Rick, who was in spirit and who did have a birthmark, made it clear to her Matt was, indeed, the one for her.

Conversely, of course, you can have a really bad or scary dream in which you see yourself in an unpleasant or even dangerous situation. That, too, ought to give you a heads-up to think about what you've been doing and maybe start to do something differently.

The information you receive in a "bad" dream
can help you to extricate yourself from a situation that may be causing you nightmares
when you're awake.

One powerful metaphoric example of this occurred when a client was having a recurrent dream in which she was stuck in a fenced-in area and couldn't get out. At the time, she was very unhappy in her job and taking a lot of undeserved grief from her boss. Then, unexpectedly, a position became available in another department, at which point my client had another dream. Now the fenced-in area had a golden gate that opened for her to walk through. When she called to ask me what it all meant, I explained that she'd been given a golden opportunity to get away from her abusive boss, and that her dream was letting her know that all she had to do was walk through the door that had opened for her. She did, and she rose in her new job to become a senior vice president of the company she worked for.

In other words, psychological dreams—if we're smart and alert enough to pay attention to them, and once we interpret them properly—can help us to determine where we ought (or ought not) to be headed in our lives. But that doesn't mean what we dream is necessarily going to happen unless we do something to make it happen—it's not the same thing as a psychic dream, which is often a premonition of things to come.

GETTING A HEADS-UP FROM THE WORLD OF SPIRIT

Very often, as I mentioned earlier, before I have a reading scheduled with a new client, someone comes to me in a dream. Sometimes that person is the client, and then, when I meet him or her, I realize that this is the person I dreamed about. He or she will be dressed the same way and say the same things as the person in my dream. And sometimes it is the person in spirit who is going to connect with the client who comes to me in my dream. What's happening in both cases is that I'm already tapping into my psychic self and making a connection even though I haven't yet met the person for whom I'll be doing the reading.

Not too long ago, I did a reading for a woman whose husband, Arthur, had passed. The night before, Arthur came through to me in a dream. In the dream, his wife was debating about whether or not to have some work done on the house, and

Arthur said, "It's a go." When the woman arrived the next day, I just looked at her and said, "You're thinking about doing some home improvements and Arthur says it's a go." She was obviously shocked and asked me why I'd say such a thing. "Because your husband told me to," I said. Apparently, "it's a go" was one of Arthur's favorite expressions, and his having spoken those words to me in my dream was his way of validating to his wife that it was really him.

But I've also had other kinds of premonitory dreams that had nothing to do with a client. The first one I remember was when I was just fifteen years old and working part-time at Brooks Brothers after school. At that time, the shop was across from Grand Central Terminal, and there was a bank on Madison Avenue where all the employees did their banking. In my dream, there was a robbery at the bank. A gunman in a hooded sweatshirt came in and made everyone lie down on the floor. He was wearing sunglasses and all I could see was the side of his face. Then, a few days later, I went to the bank to cash a check, and, as the saying goes, my dream came true, just exactly as I'd dreamed it. Luckily nobody got hurt, but I should have paid more attention to my dream!

If you experience something in a dream that doesn't make sense in your life, it may be a premonition of things to come—and sometimes you won't even realize it until you're experiencing déjà vu all over again!

Fast-forward about twenty years to another such premonitory dream. This time I dreamed I was standing outside my office. There was a distinct smell of bacon in the air, which wouldn't be unusual because there's a diner right next door, but when I looked up I saw that there were several emergency vehicles pulled up in front of the financial services center across the street. And sure enough, about two weeks later, I was standing outside my office, smelling the bacon from the diner, when several emergency vehicles pulled up in front of the financial services center, which had just had a bomb scare.

A classic example of a premonitory psychic dream involved a client who was constantly dreaming of drowning. She told me that in her dream it was as if she were in an elevator and the elevator was filling up with water. Then, one day, she was in an elevator on the basement level of a building when there was a water main break and the elevator began to fill with water, to the point where she almost drowned before being rescued. When you dream something that vividly, and certainly if you have the same dream repeatedly, it's a good idea not to ignore it.

In another instance, a gentleman had dreamed that he was being propelled from a car. He couldn't tell in the dream whether he was the driver or the passenger, but not too long after that, he was on a road trip with a friend. The friend was driving when a tractor-trailer jackknifed on the road ahead of them and they ran right into it. My client's seat belt snapped and he was thrown from the car. Luckily, he survived. Afterward, he told me that he'd been trying to decide whether or not to take that trip, and, had he been paying more attention to his dreams, he might have made a different decision. The lesson to be learned here is that not all premonitory dreams necessarily have to come true; heeding the warnings we receive from the spirit world in our dreams can help us change the outcome by making better decisions for ourselves.

There are many kinds of premonitory dreams, but one of the most common is to dream about someone who is going to pass over or to dream of a death before it occurs. One woman saw herself in a dream dressed entirely in black. Three weeks later, her brother died, and it became clear that she had been mourning him before he passed.

It's also not unusual for someone to dream about a friend or relative he or she hasn't seen in years and then to "run into" that person a few days later, or to be thinking about someone when "out of the blue" the phone rings and it's that person. Those aren't just coincidences. What happens is that we're opening ourselves up to our own soul energy, which allows us to make connections we wouldn't otherwise be making. The energy is always out there; it's just up to us to tap into it, and the easiest time for us to do that is when we're sleeping and our conscious thoughts aren't interfering with or censoring what's happening on the psychic level. That's the reason why those in the world of spirit often come to us when we're asleep.

When we're asleep our minds are open, so it's easier for the energy of those in spirit to come through.

DREAM VISITS FROM THE SPIRIT WORLD

When we receive a dream visit from someone who has passed, our loved one is there to let us know that he or she is okay and to make sure that we're okay, too.

People ask me how they can be sure that the dead person is really there and that they're not simply dreaming "about" that person. My answer is that a true dream visit is always extremely vivid and tactile. The person may touch you or kiss you or hold you, and you'll actually be able to feel the touch. After 9/11, for example, a client told me that her husband, a firefighter who died at the World Trade Center, came to her in a dream and kissed her on the cheek. She could actually feel his lips on her cheek as he came back to kiss her good-bye because he hadn't had a chance to do that before going off to work on the last morning of his life.

If your dream is unusually vivid, and especially if you can feel the touch or caress of a loved one, you're having a dream visit, not just a dream.

Sometimes, however, our dead loved ones also come to pass on information they want or need us to have. One client, for example, was in the market for a new home when she got some pretty good real estate advice from her grandmother. (You may have figured out by now that grandmas seem to be particularly caring about those they leave behind, and in this case, my client's loving grandma was also a lot more savvy than many real estate brokers I've met on this plane.) About ten years ago, well before the current real estate boom, my client's grandmother came to her in a dream and described in specific detail the house her granddaughter would be seeing. And, she added, "It's going to be a terrible mess, it's going to need major work, but whatever you do, you have to buy it. This house is going to be your security for life." Needless to say, my client found the house her grandmother had described. It was a total disaster, but she insisted on buying it, despite her family's protests, and now that house is worth several million dollars.

There are other kinds of information the spirits sometimes need to pass on. I talked earlier about the fact that it's sometimes hard for loved ones to let go and pass over when they know how difficult it will be for the ones they are leaving behind, and that it may be equally difficult for us to accept the fact that they've chosen to pass when we're not there with them. Lydia was beating herself up because she'd been on a much-needed weekend vacation with her family when her grandmother, to whom she'd been acting as caregiver, passed on. Before she left, Lydia said, her grandmother had assured her that she "wouldn't be going anywhere soon" and that she'd be just fine with her other granddaughter, Lydia's sister, who would be taking care of her while Lydia was away. Nevertheless, on the day Lydia was to return, her grandmother died, and Lydia simply couldn't release the guilt she was feeling until her grandmother came to her in a dream and said, "I wouldn't have been able to go while you were there because you wouldn't have let me, and I needed to die." I explained to Lydia that her grandmother had needed to move on, and that she had, very thoughtfully, not passed until the day

Lydia was returning anyway so as not to cut short her vacation!

On the other hand, it's also possible for a loved one to let us know, in a dream, that we'll soon be joining him or her, as was the case for a client who told me that she felt more at peace than she'd ever been before in her life. She was planning a trip when her grandmother came to her in a dream, handed her a bouquet of red roses, and told her that they would be together soon. She didn't know what to make of that, but about a month later the plane she was on, Flight 587, crashed over the Rockaways and she died.

Although it's hard to describe in specific detail, I always tell people that a dream visit from someone in spirit, while it is always extremely vivid and detailed, doesn't have to make sense. It can be very metaphoric. It may take the dead person a while to figure out exactly how to come through, so he or she may give you symbols to try to get the message (whatever it is) across.

Years ago I met a woman who had formerly been an executive at ABC News. At the time I met her, she was very ill and knew she was dying, but she wanted to help me get into television and had been determined to make it happen. After she passed, I began to dream about her. In my dreams she was taking me down a long, ornate hallway and telling me, "Now remember, when you get to the end of the hallway, that's when things are going to happen." It was her way of letting me know that she was still with me and still helping me, and just a few weeks later, I received a phone call from someone at one of the major cable networks offering me a contract for a development deal.

Another happy example of a dream message involved a client who had been told she couldn't have children. In her dream, her mother was handing her a beautiful newborn baby and telling her, "This is your daughter." Several months later, the woman was delighted to discover that she was pregnant, and she did give birth to a beautiful little girl.

Dream visits are prime time for those in spirit
to deliver messages—not just for us but also
for others here on earth.

The message, however, may be intended not for you directly but for someone else in your family. One clear example of this occurred when a client dreamed that her husband was eating chocolate and handing a piece of the chocolate to a beautiful little baby boy. The woman knew it was her husband, but she had no clue as to why he would be feeding chocolate to a baby— until, two months later, her daughter found out she was pregnant and, in due time, gave birth to a baby boy.

Most often the messages you receive are loving and reassuring, but they may also be warnings of things to come. For example, in my previous book, I talked about the Kraus sisters, Helen and Carol, whom I called the Aunts, and who helped me to accept and develop my psychic abilities. Helen died about fifteen years ago and Carol about ten. They've come to me many times in dreams just to let me know that they're okay, but I hadn't dreamed about them (or they hadn't paid me a dream visit) in quite some time when, while I was working on this book, I dreamed that I was in their house and they were telling me I was working too hard and needed to take better care of myself. At the time, I dismissed it as "just a dream," but a few days later I came down with the flu, which knocked me off my feet for almost two weeks. The interesting thing is that, when I was much younger and they were alive, they were always taking care of me as if they were my surrogate mothers. In retrospect I realize how dumb I was for not paying attention when they were so clearly just continuing the role they'd always had in my life and were still trying to take care of me.

One of the most amazing warning dreams I've ever heard about was told to me by a client. It seems that her five-year-old son had been dreaming about a man in his bedroom telling him that there was going to be a fire. When their house actually caught fire, despite what he'd been telling them about the man, the boy's parents initially thought he had set it because he knew exactly where it had started—in a faulty electrical wire in the laundry room. When I heard the story, I recommended that my client go to the town hall and see what she could find out about the history of the house. She learned that the original owner, along with his wife and two sons, had died in a grease fire in that very house more than fifty years before. It was he who had come to her son in a dream to warn him that history was about to repeat itself. His spirit had lingered in the house as a guardian and hadn't been able to go forward until, by helping my client's family, he was able to release the guilt he still had about not having been able to save his own family so that he could move on.

"Hold fast your dreams!
Within your heart
Keep one still, secret spot
Where dreams may go . . ."
—*Louise Driscoll*

WRITE IT DOWN AND FIGURE IT OUT

Because dreams of all kinds are very often so metaphorical and because we "forget" them so quickly when we awaken and the conscious mind takes over, I always tell people to keep a pad and pencil by their bed and jot down what they've dreamed as quickly as possible.

Once it's down on paper, you can go back and think about it at leisure to determine its significance, or, when something comes into your life that you dreamed would occur, you can go back and compare the dream to the reality. You can also begin to determine the significance of certain symbols that, I have found, are fairly universal in the world of dreams. My wife, for example, dreamed that she was on a sailboat when it crashed into the rocks on the shoreline, and, several weeks later, she went into the hospital to undergo major surgery. In retrospect, her dream was symbolically predicting that she would soon be experiencing a "rocky" period in her life.

Through the years, I've kept my own dream log and many of my clients have also told me their dreams and asked me to help interpret them. Based on both my own and their dream experiences, I've come to realize that particular symbols occur again and again in dreams, and that each of them always has a particular significance. In my first book I included a brief chart of the symbols that appear most often, along with their meanings. I've expanded it here to help you recognize and interpret what comes to you in your dreams.

DREAM CHART

BED

Beds always represent health.

Seeing yourself in a bed indicates that you need to pay attention to your health; usually represents a surgery or a serious, potentially life-threatening illness.

Dreaming that you are making or changing a bed means that there will be a new romantic interlude in your life.

BOOTS

New boots: Great success in your dealings. Head of household will be very successful.

Torn, old boots: Sickness in family; being stuck.

BRIDGES

Bridges that are long and winding represent coming to a pivotal point in your life. Denote total life's movement.

A damaged bridge means obstacles in all facets of life.

Coming across a bridge denotes a total change in the status of a relationship.

BUTTERFLY

Is noted in the journey of the soul at the time of death. Butterflies are connected to the idea of immortality of the soul.

Dreaming of a caterpillar becoming a butterfly means a spiritual journey.

Butterflies in flight represent completion of a union—meaning marriage.

DOVE

Most people associate the dove with Christianity. The Holy

Spirit, usually a dove, represents a very important message from a dead person, a passing, or moving on to a higher level.

DROWNING OR BEING DROWNED

Can denote loss of personal property, an impending tragedy, or death.

Dreaming of being saved by a male lifeguard represents a path toward overcoming your loss.

Finding oneself being saved by a female lifeguard denotes being a widow.

DUCKS

Ducks in a group denote a trip.

To see ducks being hunted denotes loss of a job.

Ducks flying in formation represent great fortune coming your way!

EXAMS OR TESTS

Passing means overcoming everyday obstacles; honor and courage.

FACE

Dreaming of a pale face represents an illness or a potential death.

A pimple on the face denotes dishonor or being falsely accused of a crime.

Deformities of the face represent challenges to one's honor.

FARMER

Generally, if you dream of anything related to a farmer, it's good.

A farmer harvesting his crops indicates a secure financial future.

If you're harvesting a significant crop, such as corn or wheat, it

means that you are meant for great things, such as running
for public office.

FIRE

A man's dreaming of fire means that he is afraid of intimacy
and commitment.

Fire in a festive situation, such as a campfire or a bonfire, means
that there's a new child coming into your life.

A fire in nature, such as a flash fire, represents the end of a bad
life situation—in other words, a new beginning, which is
good.

Burning out the ground can also indicate that something new is
coming, especially in business.

FISH

Dead fish indicate that major disappointments will come upon
your family.

For women, dreaming of brightly colored or tropical fish represents a successful union with a wealthy man.

FLYING

Flying through a ring of fire means that there will be a calamity
on a global scale.

Flying when someone is coming after you signifies a potential
health concern.

Dreaming that you are in flight could denote problems with a
relationship.

If you're falling during flying, you will be experiencing a significant event that causes you to spiral downward.

If you dream of being a bird in flight, you'll experience a period
of prosperity and growth.

GOD

Receiving an important message regarding your purpose in life.
An indication that you are on the right path and living your
life in a virtuous way.

HAWK

Be cautious in choosing a business partner.
A hawk can also represent jealousy and should be taken as a
warning to the type of people with whom you associate.
Death of a hawk: overcoming your opposition.

HEAVEN

Dreaming of a religious figure (such as Jesus Christ) indicates
that you've worked hard and are finally on the right path.

HELL

Represents personal turmoil that reflects some kind of misfortune in your family and for your friends. Be careful of your
path in life.

HORSES

Usually represent major good fortune.
Dreaming of a white horse indicates that you will have a major
windfall.
A dark horse means a significant change in business.
A horse bucking indicates overcoming disappointments with
friends and associates.

KISSING

A family member: lucky in love.
An enemy: making peace with a family member.
In an uncontrollable fashion: danger in your life.

LEGAL PROBLEMS
Dreaming of being a lawyer represents great career success.

Legal problems denote that you should use caution in choosing your friends or watch for dishonor among friends.

MONSTER OR VAMPIRE
People saying or spreading false rumors about you.

Watch out for things blowing out of proportion.

Watch out for people telling tall tales.

PSYCHIC (DREAMING OF)
Revealing a secret. If the information is positive, great life changes are in store for you.

If the message is negative, pay attention to details or situations in friendships.

SKINNY
Means major misfortune in health and personal matters. Watch out for your mental health.

SWEET DREAMS

Finally, you can actually "sweeten" your dreams by inviting a loved one in spirit to visit you while you sleep, but first you'll need to get yourself into the proper mind-set.

One of the biggest obstacles to receiving a dream visit from a loved one in spirit is the guilt we carry when a loved one dies. We never feel that there's a "right time" for someone to go, and we need to give ourselves permission to understand and make peace with that. I always tell my clients that they need to "clear the guilt logjam" by working with a grief counselor, and that when they're ready to let go of their residual guilt and understand that they have no responsibility for the death, their loved ones will be able to communicate with them.

Open your heart and your mind and invite
your loved ones to visit you while you sleep.

Once you've found peace within yourself, you'll be in the right mind-set to ask for a visit. When you're ready, take an item that has a very special meaning for you and your loved one—it could be a photograph, a letter, a personal possession like a hair clip or a piece of jewelry, or even a lock of hair. The reason for doing this is that there is always residual energy from the person with whom it is associated lingering in the object. Put it on your bedside table or under your pillow and, before you go to bed, speak aloud and say, "Dad [or whomever you want to visit], I need you to come and let me know you're okay." It may not happen the first night or the second, because the one in spirit will need to find the right moment and know that you're really receptive, but it will happen, and when it does, that visit can give you a sense of peace and allow you to release your grief in the knowledge that the one who has died is still with you.

SOUL PRINTS

❋ Every dream has some kind of psychic significance.

❋ What's happening in your dream can give you clues about how to handle what's happening in your life.

❋ Dreams can provide us with insights into past-life experiences.

❋ Dreams are most often metaphoric, so their significance may not always be instantly understood. Those misunderstandings can sometimes be amusing, once we figure them out.

❋ Dreams can be premonitions of things to come or warnings of things we should be trying to avoid.

❋ It's a good idea to keep a pad and pencil by your bed and to jot down your dreams as soon as you wake up so that you don't forget them and can think about what they might mean.

❋ Dream visits are different from dreaming "about" someone. They are always extremely vivid and may be symbolic.

❋ You can invite a dream visit from a loved one in spirit by getting yourself into the right mind-set just before you go to bed.

6

"Ring Around the Tub": Ghosts, Crime Scenes, and Lingering Energy

People are always asking me about ghosts and whether there's really such a thing as a house being haunted.

My experience has been that when a house is "haunted," there's a troubled soul still in residence. The dead person probably doesn't mean to make trouble for the current residents, but she is lingering, either because she doesn't realize she's dead or because she hasn't yet come to terms with the circumstances of her death.

We on this plane can get stuck when we don't come to terms with the death of a loved one, but those in spirit can also stick around to haunt us.

Earlier I talked about the fact that souls who get stuck may attach themselves to people who are troubled or vulnerable and mess with their heads. In the chapter on dreams I talked about the soul who warned the little boy about a fire that would occur in his house. But neither of these is exactly the same as a ghost.

In my experience, there are three kinds of ghosts. The first or lower-form ghost is the soul who inhabited your home at some time in the past and gets caught in a kind of limbo, repeating activities he or she engaged in while alive—almost like an old TV program stuck in a perpetual rerun. This happens mostly when the person died violently or suddenly and hasn't figured out he or she is no longer alive. Let's say you bought an old house, and the wife of the former owner had accidentally fallen off a ladder and died in the house. She might not realize she was dead and, in consequence, you might see an apparition of her in the house doing the same thing over and over again.

Not too long ago, I was asked to investigate a series of ghost sightings in a government building on Long Island. I discovered that the building had formerly been a school and the woman who had been the headmistress was still occupying the basement. This woman, whose name was Elizabeth Warren, appeared to me and immediately asked what I was doing interrupting her class. She had died suddenly of a lung infection, which at the time was probably pneumonia, and because she never realized she was dead, she had never moved on. In fact, she believed that the school was still there and that the workers in the basement were her students. She'd been trying to get them to listen to her and was trying to scold them for their bad behavior.

In fact, many old houses are full of ghosts. Recently, I filmed an episode of *Ticket,* a program on the Long Island public television station that focuses on local arts and culture. We filmed at a place called Raynham Hall, which is now a museum, housed in a building in Oyster Bay that's more than 250 years old. Raynham Hall is known to be "haunted," and I did actually have a few ghostly encounters while I was there. The first spirit to appear was a woman named Sally Townsend, who had lived in the house during the Revolutionary War. It seems that Miss Townsend had fallen in love with a British officer named Lieutenant Colonel John Simcoe, but, because he was British and, therefore, "the enemy," her family wouldn't let her marry him. She never recovered from her broken heart and had, therefore, never moved on. My second encounter was with an Irish immigrant named Michael Conlon who had worked as a servant in the house in the 1860s. And the third was a French officer who had been hanged with Benedict Arnold. His story was that he'd had an affair with the wife of a general who'd been living at Raynham Hall and who got his retribution by having the man who'd cuckolded him hanged as a spy. Each of these apparitions identified himself or herself to me so that the producers of the program were later able to verify the existence of these individuals and the validity of the information they'd given me.

"Ghosts seem harder to please than we are; it
is as though they haunted for haunting's
sake—much as we relive, brood, and smoulder
over our pasts."

—*Elizabeth Bowen*

The second kind of ghost is a poltergeist. This type of ghost has the ability to open and close doors or move the furniture. You don't actually see the poltergeist, but you do see the results of his or her activities. Poltergeists aren't dangerous, but they can be extremely annoying, especially if you keep finding things in your house rearranged so that you begin to think you're having some kind of mental breakdown. Mainly they are playful, they generally manifest themselves in ways that are energy oriented (such as turning lights on and off), and they often target children because they're more open to the world of spirit.

The third type of ghost is a regular dead person, usually a family member who decides to stick around. Particularly if the person died an unnatural death, he or she may want to communicate in order to have some kind of closure with you. He or she may also show up in a time of trouble to provide support or at a happy time to share in your celebration.

Ghosts may be disturbing, but in most cases
they don't want to harm you.

SEEING GHOSTS

"Ghosts," as most people call them, actually transfer their energy to the house itself, where they stick around like an old ring around the tub. Generally, when people call me in to clear a house of an unwanted soul, I can feel the energy as soon as I walk into a house, and it's my job to help the soul get "unstuck." I can usually do that through a combination of prayer and just communicating with the lingering spirit to let him or her know politely that he or she doesn't belong there anymore and needs to move on.

One of my most intense experiences took place in 2004 when a family called me because they were experiencing extremely strange goings-on in the rambling Victorian house on the North Shore of Long Island that they'd purchased about a year before. Doors were opening, lights were going on and off, and they were hearing footsteps when no one was walking around. There were sudden changes in temperature and strange odors with no discernible source. The family consisted of a mother and father and their three children ages eleven, nine, and seven. The seven-year-old's room, in particular, seemed to be a hotbed of unexplained activity.

When I arrived, I tuned in to the energy, as I do whenever I'm called in to visit a "haunted" house. I find that in these situations I get pulled to particular areas by what I like to think of as a kind of psychic divining rod. I was pulled to the seven-year-old daughter's bedroom and was sitting by myself on her canopied bed, surrounded by her dolls and stuffed animals, when a woman dressed in an old-fashioned high-collared dress and black shoes came in and asked me very politely if I'd like a cup of tea. I didn't know who she was, but I assumed she might be the mother or aunt of the homeowner. When my client returned, I told her that this nice elderly lady had offered me tea, and she just shook her head and said flatly, "No, she's dead."

As I started walking through the house with my clients, other "ghosts" began to show up: an old sea captain who had a full beard and used extremely colorful language, and another gentleman who, I somehow knew, was a barrister or lawyer.

As it turned out, the house had at one point been used as a funeral home before it was converted back into a private residence, and some of the ashes that had been stored in the basement were never removed or buried. As a result, there were so many dead people roaming around that it was like the Times Square subway station at rush hour. To clear the lingering negative energy and put the house back in harmony, I used a combination of prayer, sprinkling the house with holy water, and even feng shui.

I went from room to room sprinkling holy water and politely asking the spirits to leave because they were no longer welcome there. I've found that holy water, because it has been blessed, is extremely effective at replacing bad energy with energy that is positive. I also suggested moving particular pieces of furniture to change the energy of the room, which is one aspect of feng shui. Although traditional feng shui has specific rules about how to do this, I go by psychic instinct, which is what I feel when I enter a particular space.

Old houses have a history, which sometimes includes a previous tenant who hasn't yet figured out that his or her lease was up a long time ago.

Sometimes, however, people are happy to have their "friendly" ghosts stick around, as was the case for the proprietors of an old inn I visited in Vermont. The house was built in the mid-1800s, and the original innkeeper, Margaret Smith, had been a lovely, caring woman who took in travelers even when they didn't have the money to pay for their room. Now, the proprietors told me, their guests were seeing Margaret's apparition in various rooms throughout the house. Apparently her call to hospitality was so strong that she had stuck around and was still catering to "her" guests. In this instance, Margaret was completely benign—even kindly—and the innkeepers felt that their guests actually enjoyed having her around.

Most people, however, would prefer not to share their living space with former tenants in spirit, and because houses do act as repositories for the energy of people or events in the past, it's a good idea to become familiar with the history of any house you consider buying. One thing that can really start to stir up any lingering spirits is the new owners' deciding to renovate their home. Think of it as digging up and turning over the dirt in a garden. When you do that, you're disturbing all the little creatures that have been living in that soil, and they all come creeping to the surface. Personally, I discovered how much trouble those disturbed spirits can cause when I was called in to see what was going on at an old farmhouse on the North Fork of the eastern end of Long Island.

The current owners were making some renovations and one thing after another kept going wrong: One of the construction workers severed a finger; another fell off a ladder and swore that he had been pushed. But that wasn't all. They'd been experiencing strange, sometimes annoying, sometimes scary happenings for quite some time. For example, the family would come home and find the back door standing wide open even though they distinctly remembered locking it. And there was a vile odor emanating from what had once been a root cellar and was now part of the basement. They kept making excuses for all the strange goings-on—clumsy builders, faulty memory, bad pipes. But what finally convinced them to call me in was the fact that their children reported waking up in the night to find a strange figure standing in their room.

As soon as I arrived, all the lights started going on and off. The spirits were letting me know they were there and that they knew I was there, too. As I walked around, various souls started coming through. The original owner of the house, as it turned out, had been a pastor who had molested young children. When he was found out, he committed suicide in the house, but not before he'd also hanged one of his young victims there. But there was also a second, totally unrelated group of souls—a young boy, his grown-up sister, and their grandmother, all of whom had died in a fire in the house more than a hundred years after the pastor's suicide.

So, in total, there were five souls in residence, none of them aware that they were dead and didn't belong there, all of them emitting negative energy that was making a lot of trouble for the present living residents. What I was finally able to do was to negotiate with them and get them to understand that they really needed to move on and leave my miserable clients alone to get on with their own lives.

But even if your house is brand-new, the land itself has energy, so you need to be aware of what may have been standing in that spot before your new house was built. And one place you probably want to stay away from is a site that was previously a cemetery.

LINGERING SOULS AND THE ENERGY OF CEMETERIES

Very often, depending on the circumstances of their deaths, souls may not have moved on properly and instead linger near where their bodies are buried, which means that there can be a lot of psychic activity even in the most peaceful-looking cemetery.

I ran into a few of these lingering spirits when I filmed an A&E special at Sparta Cemetery in Scarborough, New York. As often happens, because we were there, the spirits were excited and wanted to talk. The caretaker took me from one grave to another and I was able to provide him with information about the person who was buried in each one. One gentleman, who had been buried near a tree somewhat separated from the other graves, came through as being rather nasty and belligerent (no doubt not much different from the way he'd been in life). He didn't at all like the idea that we were there with a camera crew bothering him, and I had to have a little talk with him about moving on.

The incident that most impressed the caretaker (and this didn't make it into the final cut of the program that eventually aired) was when I led him to the grave of a legendary figure called the Leather Man, who had roamed the area in the late 1800s and had originally been buried there in an unmarked grave until members of the Westchester County Historical Society discovered its location and had a proper marker erected during the 1930s. The reason the segment wasn't included in the program is that the Leather Man's story is so well-known throughout the area even though I had never heard of him until his spirit led me to his burial spot.

I made another on-air cemetery visit a few years ago when I was called by WB11 News. It seems that the reporter for their consumer advocate segment "Help me, Howard" had been contacted about disturbing goings-on at a local cemetery. Two night security guards had actually quit their jobs because of these strange events. As they were driving through the cemetery at night, their car would begin to shimmy or would just go dead. Lights were going on and off in the chapel; in short, all kinds of weird things were happening. When I went to check it out, I discovered that there had been a lot of vandalism occurring in the cemetery, and the souls were taking out their anger on the security guards who, so far as they were concerned, had not been doing their jobs. Even as I was there filming the segment, the wind kicked up, the clouds rolled in, and the skies began to rumble, just as if it were a horror movie. In fact, however, all these disturbances were just the result of restless souls acting out and being disruptive.

When I was a little kid, my grandmother used to take me to the Calvary Cemetery in Queens, and I loved going there because I was seeing people all the time. That happens frequently in cemeteries, and sometimes—like when I saw the ghost of the woman dressed in black in the house on Long Island—I can get confused about who's dead and who's alive.

I also believe, however, that a cemetery acts as a kind of spiritual vortex, and that being near the bodies of our loved ones in spirit makes it easier for us to call upon and communicate with them.

Personally, I find cemeteries to be very peaceful, but at times, as I've said, there can be troubled souls disturbing the peace. Like the ghosts in haunted houses, they may be the souls of people who died suddenly or who died as the result of a crime or an act of violence. In fact, for that very reason, I worry about whatever is going to be built on the site of the World Trade Center. I believe that in a place where so many souls went out so violently and suddenly, there's bound to be a great deal of residual energy sticking around that could cause problems later on.

JEFFREY THE PSYCHIC DETECTIVE

In New York State there is now a law that requires the disclosure of any crime committed in a house that's on the market—which could mean that the soul of the victim is still there or that there is negative energy clinging to the crime site.

Anyone who's watched the hit television series *Medium*, which is based on an actual person, knows that there are, in fact, psychic detectives who help the police solve particularly puzzling crimes. Truthfully, I suspect there may be many more psychics working with the police than the public is aware of.

If you're wondering, "How do they do that?" the best way I know to explain it is that crime scenes, like haunted houses, have residual energy. I can feel that energy and get a sense of where it's coming from. I think everyone can do that on some level. You may have experienced it if you've been in a place that just felt creepy to you even though you didn't know why. The only difference is that I'm able to tune in to the source of the creepy feeling and determine its cause.

When I do that, I can "rerun" the crime on a psychic level, and the quicker I get there, the more powerful the energy is. In addition, the more people there have been at the scene leaving their own energy, the more confusing it becomes—there are so many footprints that it's hard to tell which ones belong to whom, only in this case they are psychic footprints. More often than not, however, I'm not called in until the police have run out of all other possible leads. The call usually goes something like, "Jeffrey, I'm at a dead end here. Can you help me out?"

Very recently, for example, *The Maury Show* asked me to go to Cleveland to participate in a program about missing children. When I arrived, I was shown a picture of a young girl but wasn't given any information about her. I later learned that the girl's name was Gina, she had been missing for more than a year, and she was just a month past her fourteenth birthday when she disappeared. She was last seen leaving her middle school, and the tracking dogs that had been brought in lost her scent just a block from the school. A surveillance video from one of the local businesses had caught her on tape talking to an unidentified male. The FBI was called in on the case, but she had never been found.

In this instance, I was taken to Gina's home, and before I even got inside, I was beginning to perceive the scene as if I were looking through the perpetrator's eyes. I could "see" that whoever it was knew the neighborhood well and had been in the area at least six or seven months. Then I was looking through Gina's eyes, and I could see her talking with the person who had taken her as if she knew him. He was a black male, in his late twenties to early thirties, and he had facial hair. I also saw a light blue compact car.

When I spoke with Gina's understandably distraught parents, I was able to tell them that she was definitely alive. And when I described the man and the car, it turned out that the FBI had been looking for a person and a car of exactly those descriptions.

The parents were then interviewed on the air, and the father described what I had been able to tell them as "remarkable." I know they were comforted by the fact that I had stated unequivocally that Gina was alive—especially since the other information I had given them matched so exactly what the authorities already knew.

While I was there, I also began to get information about another girl who had disappeared just five blocks from where

Gina went missing, and I was convinced that the two situations were related. Based on what I told them, the FBI is, as I'm writing this, following up on the leads I was able to give them.

I know the information I provided was very helpful to Gina's parents. I'm happy for that, but I also know that if I'd been brought in earlier, when the trail was fresh, I'd have been able to do even more. In these situations, I think of myself as a psychic bloodhound following a scent. The longer it is between the time the crime is committed and the time I'm called in, the less residual energy there is left at the scene and the more new energy has covered up the original psychic "scent."

Those in spirit know that helping us to solve
a crime will bring the kind of closure that
allows us to move on with our lives.

Not too long ago, I was in the middle of a book tour when the owner of a bookshop where I was doing a signing asked me to help find out what had happened to her friend, who had been brutally murdered in another shop around the corner. The victim's spirit was still lingering in the shop because her death was so violent and sudden that she hadn't yet realized she was dead and, therefore, hadn't gone across. She was able to give me details about how the crime was committed that I couldn't possibly have known and that convinced the police of the validity of other information she gave me about the attacker, including what he looked like and his psychological profile. At the point when I had to move on to the next stop of my tour, the authorities were following the leads I had given them. I wish I'd been able to do more, but, unfortunately, I simply didn't have the time.

In another recent incidence, I was called to the scene of a murder for which the police couldn't find any point of entry. They suspected that the perpetrator was someone who had worked for the victim and had a key, but all the employees had airtight alibis.

In this case, I was able to contact the victim's deceased husband, who let me know that, many years before, he'd been a bit of a philanderer and had left a key outside the back door so that he could let himself in late at night without disturbing his wife. As it turned out, a delivery person who regularly came to the back door had discovered the key still hidden there and had used it to gain entrance and commit the crime.

Not all the crimes I'm called in on are murders, however. I've also helped to solve a jewel theft, and once I was asked to find an embezzler. In that case, the owner of the business brought me in undercover as a "consultant" to figure out who had been stealing from him. You might not think of a place of business as a crime scene, but in this case that's exactly what it was. And, as in any crime scene, there was an energy trail to follow, like a psychic trail of evidence. I was able to follow the energy trail that eventually led me to its source—the embezzler.

MURDER OR SUICIDE—NOT ALWAYS THE ANSWER YOU WANT

Nobody ever wants to believe that a loved one has committed suicide. In fact, there's so much anger, guilt, and shame attached to the one who survives the suicide of a loved one that it, probably along with incest, remains one of the few subjects nobody wants to discuss. In many religions suicide is considered a sin against the sacredness of life. But even when religion isn't an issue, the survivor is bound to feel that he or she could or should have been able to prevent it.

Sometimes I'm able to alleviate the survivor's pain by helping to prove that what is being called a suicide was, in fact, a crime. One such occasion that remains vivid in my mind involved a young man who was found in his car shot in the head with the gun still in his hand. Because he had preexisting psychological problems, the police termed his death a suicide and didn't investigate any further, but the man's parents didn't believe it. In this case, the victim himself came through and let me know that there had been someone else in the car who shot him and then put the gun in his hand to make it look like a suicide. I was able to tell the young man's parents the killer's name and describe what he was wearing. In addition, there were no powder burns on the victim's hand, which would suggest that he had not, in fact, shot himself, but since the police were so convinced that it was a suicide, they hadn't really looked into all the evidence as thoroughly as they might have. Based on the information I provided, they reopened the case and were able to make an arrest.

In that situation, I not only helped to take a killer off the street, I also relieved the victim's parents of the grief and guilt they felt at having their son's death termed a suicide. Sometimes, however, a death really is a suicide, and no matter how much the survivors want to believe otherwise, there's nothing I can do to prove it wasn't. All I can do then is to help them work through the negative emotions that are preventing them from accepting the truth, forgiving the person who took his or her own life, and moving on with their own.

> It's the job of a detective—psychic or otherwise—to get to the truth, and the truth isn't always what people want to hear.

Such was the case of a woman who came to me because she simply couldn't accept the fact that her only son had killed himself. He was found hanging in his own apartment, and she was convinced that his death was a result of rough sex and that his girlfriend was somehow involved. When her son came through, he let me know not only how he had done it but also that, on his father's side of the family, back in the old country, his grandfather and one of his brothers had both suffered from depression and also hanged themselves. Being an extremely proud woman who still adhered to traditional values and who, therefore, took particular pride in her only son, my client found the truth extremely difficult to live with, even though I tried to explain to her that, in my experience, most people who commit suicide simply lose touch with reality and aren't really aware of what they're doing.

IT'S NOT ABOUT THE PSYCHIC

Anytime I'm working with people to resolve grief, find their true soul paths, or move on with their lives, I'm taking on an enormous responsibility and acting from a position of trust. But that trust and responsibility become all the more potent and important when I'm helping to solve a crime. I'm responsible to the victim's family as well as to the police and even to any potential suspect the police might track down as a result of the information I provide. It would be easy to start patting myself on the back and saying, "Aren't I great, the police couldn't find the criminal and I could. That'll show them!" Or, "See, I told you so! And you didn't want to believe me!" But that's about the worst thing I could possibly do. Not only would I be betraying the responsibility and trust I'd been given but also, if I let my ego get in the way, I wouldn't be able to do this most important work effectively.

In this kind of work, probably more than in any other aspect of what I do, I have to keep in the forefront of my mind that it's not *ever* about the psychic!

SOUL PRINTS

- ❊ Ghosts are most often troubled souls who don't realize they're dead.
- ❊ When a house is "haunted," it's because a spirit has transferred his or her energy to the house itself.
- ❊ You can clear that energy through prayer, ritual, and communicating to the spirit that he or she doesn't belong and is no longer welcome there.
- ❊ Because houses have residual energy, it's a good idea to find out about the history of any house you're planning to move into.

* Souls sometimes linger near their bodies, which means that cemeteries can be hotbeds of psychic activity—and a lot less peaceful than they look.

* Any place that was the site of a crime can have a lot of negative energy.

* Psychic detectives work by tapping in to the energy of the crime scene to get a sense of what happened.

* Just as a crime scene can be corrupted by physical disturbances, so can it be confused by too many "psychic footprints," which is why it's always easiest for a psychic to work if he or she is called in as quickly as possible.

* Sometimes survivors don't really want to know the truth— they'd rather believe a loved one was murdered than that he or she committed suicide.

* Anyone acting as a psychic detective must honor the fact that he or she is taking on an enormous amount of responsibility and is being put in a position of trust by people who are at their most vulnerable.

7

Getting People All the Help They Need

I hope that by now everyone understands why I do the work I do. It's not a parlor trick, and it's not just to prove that I can. I know that what I do can and does help all kinds of people. Throughout this book I've been mentioning that, in some cases, I recommend that my clients see a therapist to work through ongoing issues I can't resolve for them. Over the years I've developed relationships with several therapists because I have realized that we can help many more people by combining our talents. Working this way requires a great deal of open-mindedness on both sides, respect on the part of each of us for the other's professionalism, and, speaking for myself, a tremendous sense of responsibility.

THE THERAPEUTIC DOOR SWINGS BOTH WAYS

When I do a reading for someone and see that he or she is constantly making the same mistakes, I refer that person to a therapist, tell him or her what needs to be worked on, and ask him or her to come back when the therapeutic work is finished. Therapists, on the other hand, might refer a patient to me to supply a final piece of the therapeutic puzzle or to get to the source of an issue that might take months if not years of therapy to uncover.

If you keep an open mind, information you receive on a soul level can help you to discover the sources of issues that prevent you from moving forward in your life.

Once I am able to get to the source of the problem, it becomes that much easier for the therapist to help his or her patient to reach a resolution. That's a basic tenet of psychotherapy: If you don't know why you're engaging in nonproductive thoughts or behaviors, you won't be able to change them; uncover the source of the problem and you'll be able to resolve it.

When a therapist and I work together, however, it is always at arm's length, and we are extremely conscious of the necessity to preserve the privacy and confidentiality of the people we see. Without that degree of separation, the therapist would be violating the doctor/patient relationship. Furthermore, whatever information I am able to provide could be called into question if the client thought the therapist was "briefing" me in advance. Because our clients trust us, they understand that neither of us would ever undermine our credibility or—even more important—put their healing in jeopardy by breaking that trust, which is to us a sacred bond.

WHEN IT'S TIME TO CALL FOR HELP

One thing I don't want is for people to become obsessively dependent on me. I've already said that I can't control anyone else's life, so when I see that people are calling and calling, wanting me to make every decision for them, that's a signal for me to refer them to a therapist.

As with everything in life, it's good for the psychic to know when it's time to ask for help.

When clients return to me after doing the therapeutic work, I can see how much they've grown. In many cases they come back periodically for what I like to call a psychic tune-up. Additionally, a therapist might even suggest that a patient check back in with me to provide some insight into a new issue that arises during one of their sessions.

There are a variety of circumstances in which I might suggest therapy to a client. Given the nature of my work, getting stuck in bereavement is, of course, one of the most common. But I also refer people with relationship problems I can't resolve and those who are unable to break destructive patterns they've inherited from their parents or from a past-life trauma. The nature of the problem also dictates which of the several therapists I work with I'll recommend.

On that note, I thought it would be interesting to let you hear from a few of the therapists I currently work with so that they can tell you, from their point of view, how they work, how we work together, and what contribution I make to the work they do.

Dr. Holly Shaw—When the World
of Spirit Can Provide a "Missing Link"

Holly Shaw works with all kinds of patients but has a particular expertise in the area of trauma and bereavement counseling. She also works with many children and adolescents and is, as she puts it, "a kid specialist." I'll let her tell you something about herself, how we met, and how we work together.

"I was trained in a very classical, traditional manner. During my undergraduate and early graduate school years, spirituality was looked upon as something very unscientific and unprofessional, and was not regarded as having any place or meaning in our work. Later on, as I was doing my doctoral work, I was learning more and more about metaphysical issues and the part spirituality could play in grief and healing. I began to recognize the need for a dimension the professional science didn't seem to supply.

"At about the same time, I was working with several clients—one was a young widow about thirty years old—who had seen Jeffrey. Truthfully, I was uneasy about how vulnerable these people were and what this might be about, because they all spoke of him with great regard and very significant anticipation. Understandably, I think, I was afraid that this was something (or someone) that might take advantage of them or that would disrupt our own work. I made an appointment with Jeffrey because I wanted to check him out. I didn't tell him why I was there, but I think now that he probably knew.

"Before I even sat down, he began to say things about me that were absolutely accurate. This was many years ago, and at the time I was working on a very complicated grant proposal for a project I'd designed. Jeffrey described it to me so accurately that I kept looking down at the floor to be sure he wasn't reading the papers that were in the briefcase at my feet. But the briefcase was closed. I was the only one who knew the details of the whole project, so I was really impressed and, frankly, somewhat astonished.

"Since then many people have told me how astonished they were by what Jeffrey was able to tell them virtually immediately. I think that's one thing that sets him apart from a lot of the people who do this work. Another is the fact that he doesn't allow people to become overly dependent on him. People could easily see him every week or every month, but he doesn't encourage that or even allow it. He has a level of integrity that's easy to identify, and for someone like me that's very reassuring.

"If I had to describe our relationship, I guess I'd say we collaborate spiritually. We don't speak back and forth except retrospectively and we don't work together with clients. Generally, I take what the person brings to me from him and work with that. Every once in a while the person will ask me to listen to the tape of his or her reading because there's something on it he doesn't understand or wants me to clarify. It's an odd collegial relationship but one that includes trust and respect on both our parts and acknowledgment by each of us for the skills of the other. Having a client work with both of us provides a fuller experience than either of us could provide alone—although this is probably more striking for me than it is for Jeffrey.

"In the beginning, getting to the point where I'd recommend that a client see Jeffrey was much more arduous than it is now. I'd be waiting for the client to raise the issue. But now, because I'm so aware of the contribution he can make, I'm much more spontaneous about recommending him and much more astute about identifying those circumstances when that contribution will be significant, just as I help my patients to identify any of the other available resources that will contribute to their healing.

The therapist needs to be intuitive about the
kind of help a patient needs and will be willing
to accept.

"I see people who are dealing with enormously sad
things—people who've lost their entire family in a car crash, kids
who've lost parents, suicide survivors—really catastrophic events,
so I *have* to encourage them to use every resource available in body,
mind, and spirit. Jeffrey may not know this, but these days I think I
probably recommend more people to him than he does to me.

"One person he did refer to me was a woman who came
up to him at a book signing. As she later told me, she'd started to
ask a question, but before the words were even out of her mouth
he said, 'You need to see Dr. Holly Shaw. You really need to call her
tomorrow. She can help you and your daughters, and if you can't
find her number call my office. You really need to see her right
away.' When I spoke to her, the woman was understandably confused; she didn't have any idea who I was, but she did call. It
turned out that she had two daughters, one eighteen and the other
about ten or eleven. Her first husband, the father of her older
daughter, had died in a plane crash. She'd remarried, and her second husband, the biological father of her younger daughter, had
also raised the older one as his own. Then he was hit by an oil
truck and killed. So the woman had lost two husbands; the older
daughter, two fathers; and the younger one, her biological father—all to tragic accidents. Jeffrey had obviously seen this when
she approached him at the signing and knew that because of my
bereavement work I would be able to help the family.

"In another case, however, I referred a patient to him because I knew he was the one who could supply the piece that would complete her healing. My patient was a girl in her teens whose father had died before she was born of a particular genetically linked medical condition that had also taken the lives of several other family members. My patient had inherited the condition as well, but she is being treated and has an excellent prognosis. Consider her situation, however: She's inherited a potentially life-threatening medical condition from a father she never met, and because that same condition has taken the lives of so many family members, she really has no one to talk to about him.

"Her mother is wonderful and extremely devoted to her daughter, but the girl, as she was growing up, often had the feeling that she didn't want to talk about him very much. When she came to me, this young woman had many, many unanswered questions. She also had a sense of incompleteness that was almost physical. She was a competitive athlete, and she told me that all through high school she would look up into the stands, see her mom (which was good), see her opponents' families, and the strength would drain from half her body.

"Over the years we've done some really good work filling in the picture of who her father was and who he would have become so that she could better understand who she was and would become, but she had never actually *experienced* him. She was an outstanding student as well as an athlete, and she'd always been saddened that he never knew about her accomplishments. She went from wanting to know about him to wanting very much that he know about her. That wasn't anything I could give her, which is why I referred her to Jeffrey.

Sometimes a psychic can supply a kind of information and validation to which a therapist has no direct access.

"What he was able to do for her is really remarkable. Not only was he able to tell her a lot about her father, but also he was able to let her know how her father was with her—that he does see her, he supports her, and he can be there for her in a spiritual way when she needs him. Jeffrey's ability to give her that had a truly substantial impact on her ability to feel her father's presence in her life. It led to a sense of completeness that's very deep and meaningful to her. No one else could have provided what he did, and it's had a profound effect on her overall well-being and mental health.

"Both these patients were dealing with the emotional and psychological fallout of tragic deaths, but when I was looking through my client list recently to refresh my memory about people Jeffrey and I had worked with together, it struck me how many of them were suicide survivors.

"We tend to think of people who kill themselves as very depressed, and sometimes that's the case, but often it's not the case. Current research has found that there also appears to be a very strong genetic link that no one's really been able to explain except to say that it's a learned behavior—because you know it's happened in your family the taboo is lifted and it becomes more acceptable. But that's never really quite explained it to me, especially since many people who commit suicide never knew it had happened in their family. It's also been thought that the genetic link was to depression, but new research shows that folks who commit suicide don't necessarily have the genetic link to depression but do have a link to aggressive, impulsive behavior.

"Suicide, in other words, is sometimes a very impulsive act that leaves many unanswered questions. This information has not, however, reached clinicians or the general public, so survivors—not just parents but extended family, friends, teachers, etc.—are still going with traditional patterns of belief that teach us to look for the hidden clues, which, it is assumed, the person has been giving for a long time. It is, of course, agonizing to think there were subtle signs you could have picked up on to prevent it, but in my experience this is true in only a minority of cases. Yes, some suicides have struggled with depression for a long time, but for most of them, especially adolescents, it's an impulsive decision that's exactly as Jeffrey says—the person just snaps.

"I can suggest that to people and explain it's what the research literature says, but I don't have the data to convince them. So when Jeffrey says it and can tell the person in a very personal way because he's getting it from the suicide directly, that does something enormous for the survivor.

"The other part of the old theory of suicide was that it's a hostile act, and that's certainly a factor in some cases, but not always. Usually what happens is that there's great regret on the part of the person who's gone—'I didn't think, I'm sorry, I should have known, I'm sorry I hurt you.'

Information the psychic gives can change the way a survivor remembers and connects to the person who has passed.

"When Jeffrey explains the sense of remorse the person in spirit is feeling, it's very important, because otherwise families feel it was the person's intention to make them suffer and then they feel they have to continue to suffer and that it's not right for them to heal. They can't give up the grief; they don't want to be happy. This is survivor's guilt and it happens quite frequently with siblings—'It's not fair that my sister lost her life and I didn't, so I'm not entitled to fully live my life.'

"This occurs to some degree with all grieving, but it's exaggerated when it's an unnatural death that doesn't fit with our assumptions about how things ought to be. Parents, for example, know it's their job to ensure the safety and well-being of their child and if they are unable to do that, they've failed—and this is equally true if the death is from cancer or an accident or suicide. As a result, they may believe they're not entitled to live without the pain. Their child has died and they weren't able to prevent it, so this is their penance, their punishment. They don't deserve to enjoy life. Beyond that, however, even people who don't blame themselves find it inconceivable that they could ever be happy again. The pain is so huge that it seems incompatible with human life.

"The stakes are really high in these situations because these are not folks who just go through life sad; these are folks who sabotage whatever happiness they might have. If it's a youngster, it could be by doing drugs or acting out in a myriad of ways, but even parents often get into problems like this, or they're unable to parent their remaining children. When that happens, the surviving kid is likely to think, 'I know I lost my brother, but I didn't think I'd be losing my parent, too.'

"When Jeffrey can say to them, 'You're wasting the life

you have and that's not a tribute to your deceased loved one; your relative says you should do this, you should be happy,' etc., that gives them a kind of permission I cannot. When Jeffrey can give them the truth from the point of view of the deceased, it completes the picture, and they can come to new conclusions about what happened, about themselves, and about the future. That's something that's enormously valuable and meaningful and provides a sense of comfort and direction. At that point we can then begin to work on reconstructing their lives in a way that really works.

"The other aspect of this is that sometimes the pain and the grief are the person's only connection with the deceased. They say that their grief is what makes them feel closest to their loved one, it's how they remember him or her, and if they give it up they'll be abandoning him—which is, of course, anathema to them. They have to stay heartbroken and grief stricken or else, they believe, they'll forget about him, so the grief and dysfunction are perpetuated. Therapists and patients can spend years talking about this issue.

"By actually representing the deceased, who always seems to have a very specific message, Jeffrey is able to provide them with a different kind of connection so that their connection is no longer with the pain. He makes it possible for the survivors to go from the pain and the dysfunction created by that pain to experiencing the connection in a more positive way, and that frees them up to have a life. I can deal with all this in psychological terms, I can explain it, I'm very proactive, but I can't give it to them from the horse's mouth, so to speak.

"Over the years I've been constantly amazed by the many different ways Jeffrey's gift has proved profoundly beneficial to so many different people. In every case we've worked on during our interesting—and I believe mutually beneficial—collaboration from a distance, his contribution to the healing process has been extremely valuable."

INSIGHTS FOR THE PSYCHIC

Since Holly and I don't actually discuss the clients we refer to one another, and we certainly don't discuss the specific details of our work, I wasn't really aware, until I asked her to provide her perspective for this book, that current scientific research appears to be supporting my own experiences of people who'd committed suicide. While I don't require that kind of validation to know what is true and what isn't, it's as fascinating for me to have this insight into Holly's work as I hope and believe it is for her to understand what it is that I do and the healing contribution I am able to make.

SANDY RAFMAN—A TRADITIONALIST WHO KEEPS AN OPEN MIND

Sandy may be the most traditional of all the therapists with whom I work regularly. She's a psychologist and psychotherapist with a general practice, and I like to think that we each have a great deal of respect for the other's work. I am happy that Sandy appears to agree.

"I have a lot of faith in Jeffrey. I'd gone to him myself many years ago when I was just entering the field of social work. He gave me some very good readings, and I respected the quality of his work. As a result, I never had any reservations about referring people to him, but I don't talk to them about it unless the patient brings it up first. When I know someone's interested, I give him Jeffrey's number, and it's up to the patient to call. Jeffrey works the same way. Over the last number of years, he's referred clients to me and it's always the client who calls, never Jeffrey. I do call to thank him for the referral, but that's the extent of the conversation.

A therapist needs to know that the patient will be comfortable with the idea before recommending that he or she consult a psychic.

"I wouldn't say there's any one specific kind of situation that would lead me to refer a patient to him, and the ones he refers to me also are dealing with a variety of different issues. I'm trained analytically, which means I work psychodynamically. I work with my patients not just to change their behavior but to understand how their lives are impacted by what's going on, and I try to individualize the way I work to fit the patient's needs.

"One woman I'd been seeing for some time had lost a younger sister four or five years before and was still having a great deal of difficulty with the mourning and grieving process. She was also having problems with her ex-husband and her sons, and she asked me if I knew a psychic she could see. We discussed it, and when I asked what she hoped to get out of it, she told me she hoped he would be able to contact her sister and also to tell her what he saw for her boys and her life. She needed to know what she was going to be dealing with. Jeffrey did two readings with her, both of which were very on-target and very helpful. He was also able to give her messages from her sister that were very, very good for her to hear.

Having some idea of what the future may
hold can be very helpful to people in dealing
more productively with the present.

"Over the years I've had several patients who were dealing with difficult relationships and needed to have some idea of what the future held for them. They've come back from Jeffrey with some pretty positive feedback, and it usually helps our work because I get new insights from something he brings up and we are then able to work on that.

"He can see things it's not always easy to get to with a once-a-week patient. Yes, it might come out eventually, but then again it might not. We don't really know that.

"From Jeffrey's point of view, although I know—both from my own experience and from what my patients tell me—that he is extremely insightful, if he thinks someone needs more ongoing therapy, he'll refer the client to me or to another therapist. There have been numerous patients he's referred for many different reasons. One I remember was a gay man who had never really received the kind of validation he'd wanted from his mother. After I'd worked with him for a while to get through the mourning and grieving and acceptance, he went back to Jeffrey and got a very good reading. And he also became involved in a very good relationship—which was something Jeffrey had predicted, although it didn't happen as quickly as my patient would have liked!

"So, as I've said, I'm very comfortable referring people to Jeffrey, but I first have to feel that they're truly open and are going to be accepting of it. I have strong beliefs and I'm a pretty grounded person, and I also know other therapists who've been to Jeffrey and have tremendous respect for him. But there are people who just don't understand what he does, and I'm not here to tell them what to believe."

THE PSYCHIC SECONDS THE MOTION

Once again, the therapist and the psychic are in total agreement. As I've already said, I'm not here to make people believers any more than Sandy is. I may believe that their lives would be richer and more rewarding if they were able to set aside their fears of the unknown, but I'm not going to waste my time or theirs by trying to get them to see the light when they've clearly chosen to stay in the dark. Not to sound callous, but it just means these are souls who'll be coming around one more time to learn a lesson they haven't yet been able to grasp. When it comes to fulfilling your soul path, there's no such thing as social promotion.

DR. DEBORAH WOLF—THERAPIST AND SPIRITUAL SEEKER

Of all the therapists I work with, Dr. Deborah Wolf, based on her training and interests, would probably appear to be the most obvious "fit."

"There's a spiritual underpinning to the way I work that's different from other, more traditional therapists. My training is unconventional. I have a master's degree in folklore, a doctorate in psychological anthropology, and three years of postdoctoral work in medical anthropology. I've also had three years of training at an institute in integrative therapy and four years of supervision with a psychoanalyst. I've worked with Native American elders and healers, with shamans in Peru, and with Tibetan practitioners. I've tried to open myself to as many ways as possible of doing this work so that when someone comes in I have a way of working with him or her that fits the person's background.

Therapy comes in many forms, and adding a spiritual element to the purely psychological can help people discover their true path.

"The way my relationship with Jeffrey started is actually sort of amusing and very much in keeping with the way we both work. At the time, I was working with an alternative doctor whose wife knew Jeffrey and who didn't want her husband to refer patients to me for therapy until Jeffrey had given me his stamp of approval. So I went to Jeffrey for a reading, and he told me there was an ancient Chinese man standing right behind my left shoulder. Then he called out to his receptionist and told her to send people from Manhattan to me.

"After that Jeffrey started to refer people periodically. One of his referrals was a woman who'd gone to see him because she simply couldn't decide which of two men she should marry and was in a state of panic. Generally, in this kind of situation, the person hasn't been able to get in touch with who he or she really is or with her life pattern, and Jeffrey is able to see that. In this case, he told her what he saw down the road depending on which of the men she chose. Based on what he told her, she knew she had karmic issues to work out with one of them, but it just so happened that this guy was actually psychotic!

A therapist can help to ground and interpret information that's obtained on the soul or psychic level.

"When she came to see me, we worked a great deal on teaching her relaxation techniques and trying to get her in touch with her intuition on a spiritual level so that she could discover who her guides were and what she was really meant to be. Once she was able to see her own soul pattern, she could look at the patterns of each of the men in her life and see how they matched her own.

"One of her biggest problems was that she was feeling very responsible for the guy with whom Jeffrey had told her she had karmic issues, so we talked about the fact that there were ways to resolve those issues without her actually having to marry him. She could, for example, set boundaries that would make him stronger, whereas if she married him she would simply be reinforcing the very same karmic patterns she was trying to resolve. She needed to understand that the most important issue was what would be in the best interest of the development of her soul. With that kind of understanding she was able to get a much better sense of what her choice really meant.

"In the end, she married the guy who was not psychotic and they came to me for a joint session during which we talked about how they could be in relationship with one another in ways that would really build both of them together. Even though we never actually discussed it, I think that when Jeffrey sent her to me he believed I would help to open her up, deepen her, and give her a better sense of her own spiritual and intuitive power. Essentially, this is what I do with all my patients: I try to reinforce ways they can work with their own spirit and their own vision—essentially with their own soul.

A psychic can "jump-start" the healing process by giving the therapist information it might otherwise take a long time to bring to the surface.

"Because of what he does, Jeffrey can give me a starting place for therapy, and that's what I count on him for. He will have seen the pattern and will have told the client what it is, and I can then work with the person based on what he's seen. He rarely talks to me about the people he refers, but sometimes the patient will say that Jeffrey would like me to call him to get some background information. Usually I just count on what my patients tell me because I know how Jeffrey sees things, and based on what they say he's told them, I can pick up from there.

"The one time I remember differing with him was about a client's boyfriend. I think he was absolutely right in terms of how he read the guy's character, but from a therapeutic point of view I was able to see the particular function the guy played in the client's life. This is one time when we did talk, and he came around to understand that she needed that particular boyfriend at that particular time because of what was happening in her life.

"What I deal with every day is helping people to open up their soul patterns in order to resolve deep, spiritual, underlying issues. Every morning when I come in I pray that this is a sacred place where people will find healing and inspiration, and I ask to be a mirror in which they can see the strength within themselves. Then I ask if anything is being asked of me today. Because I begin the day with that kind of energy, I think people sense when they come in that this is a different kind of space. In many ways Jeffrey is an inspiration for me and certainly for the people who see him on a regular basis. I feel that he and I are working together very closely. And that modifies to some extent what I would do on my own because I ask a patient what Jeffrey says and then we can weave that into what we're working on. I've always felt tremendously privileged that he's in my life and in the lives of these people."

A Tribute to the Power of Prayer

It's very gratifying for me to know that Deborah begins her workday much as I do, by connecting with a higher power and with her higher self. I don't know how she prays or whom or what she prays to, but, as I hope I've made clear by now, it doesn't matter. What matters is that we ask to be given the wisdom that's available to all of us to discover and nurture our soul path.

The Door to Healing Swings Both Ways

One thing that's become clearer even to me from what Holly, Sandy, and Deborah have to say about their work is that my own contribution truly helps them to enhance their patients' ability to heal, which is also what their work is able to do for the people who come to me stuck, scared, and shut off from their own inner truth.

SOUL PRINTS

* There's more than one way to heal and more than one way to discover your true path. When it's a question of moving to a higher level of soul consciousness, we should seek help from whatever sources are available to us.

* Integrity and trust must be the basis for any kind of mental or emotional healing.

* Because they're so attuned to the mysterious workings of the mind, even the most traditional therapists may be very open to accepting what comes to us from the world of spirit.

* Sometimes a psychic has direct access to information it could take a therapist months or years to obtain in more traditional ways.

* Whether you're a therapist or a psychic, your first and only obligation is to do whatever is in the best interest of the client.

* Psychics and therapists are both healers and seekers of truth.

8

When Tragedy Strikes
on a Global Scale

Up to this point I've been talking mainly about personal interactions between individuals on this plane and their loved ones in spirit, and about what each one of us can do to tap in to our personal soul map. In the past several years, however, it's become clear that global events—whether planned by man or imposed by nature—can and do have life-changing effects on large groups of humanity. When that happens, the issues I've been discussing throughout this book—overcoming our fears, discovering our true path, making peace with the whole life-and-death process—are not only mirrored and magnified but also often more difficult to understand and accept.

CHALLENGES, ON WHATEVER LEVEL, ARE ALWAYS OPPORTUNITIES FOR GROWTH

While it's certainly difficult for most people to deal with violence or tragedy on a personal level, it becomes all the more difficult when the violence or tragedy occurs on a massive scale. That may be easier to do if we can just remember that these events also present opportunities for spiritual growth.

Look upon life's challenges as opportunities
for growth.

What we see as spiritual or emotional obstacles are put in our path because we're supposed to learn from them. Some people rise to the occasion and others, unfortunately, still refuse to listen and learn, no matter how loud, violent, and deadly the wake-up call may be.

RISING TO THE CHALLENGE OF NATURE

As I'm writing this in the early fall of 2005, Hurricane Rita is battering the Texas-Louisiana border just weeks after the devastation of Hurricane Katrina. In the wake of such natural disasters, heroes and antiheroes emerge. I'm sure all of us can recall at least one story we watched on television of an unlikely leader emerging from the thousands of regular people who were directly affected by these manifestations of Nature's power—someone who went out of his or her way to help a neighbor, someone who deliberately put himself or herself in harm's way in order to rescue a total stranger. I remember particularly an elderly woman who had lost everything and was living in a shelter where there were also hundreds of little children. Within a day she had all the little kids calling her Grandma. She had put aside her own losses and was focusing on whatever she could do to cheer them up and help them to overcome their fears. And we also saw images of those who took the chaos of the situation as an opportunity for personal gain or to profit from the misfortune of others. People's lives are always challenged by these disasters, and when that happens, consciousness changes. I believe that these natural disasters are Nature's way of throwing us into a learning situation, and, as with everything that comes at us in life, it's up to us to learn from it or not.

One thing we always hear after people lose their homes or possessions in an earthquake or a fire or a flood is, "You can always replace material things. What really matters is that your family is okay." But without that cataclysmic event, these people may never even have considered that truth. Their perspective on what's really important was changed. It's not that they weren't spiritual before the event; it's just that they hadn't been paying much attention to their own spirituality until Nature woke them up and gave them the opportunity to grow on a spiritual level.

And then again, there are always the people who don't want to hear the wake-up call, even when they're given fair warning. They know they have to deal with the situation, but they don't. When they're told to evacuate, they refuse to move, preferring to play Russian roulette and dare Nature to kill them.

Nature has its own system of checks and balances; for every devastation there is also a rebirth.

But natural disasters are also Nature's way of "clearing space" for a new beginning. This process of renewal can be traced all the way back to the biblical story of Noah. God (or the higher power, or nature, or however you choose to name it) was purifying the world, creating a spiritual cleansing on a global scale. Think, for example, about the terrible forest fires that occur so often in the West; if you look at those burnt-out areas a few years later, they are already coming back to life. And what we need to remember is that when people die in these circumstances, it's because these souls have chosen this way to go out. So in that sense, they, too, are part of the renewal process, whether we choose to recognize it or not.

WHEN HUMANS ACT INHUMANLY

Man-made disasters also are learning experiences, but unlike those imposed by nature they are manifestations of a karmic shift on a global scale. Karma, as I've said, is based on the law of cause and effect. While we may not be able to control another person's action, we can control our reaction to it. If someone perpetrates a violent action, we can react violently and so perpetuate the cycle of violence, or we can choose, as the Buddhists would say, to get off the wheel of karma, react in a different way, and, therefore, break the cycle. As I've been saying all along, we can make things happen in our lives, and when they don't happen, we're the ones who are holding things up.

Consider, for example, the shootings at Columbine that so shocked the nation. The kids who created this massacre were outsiders, "different," misunderstood, and, yes, they were marginalized, teased, and bullied by at least some of their classmates.

But how did they choose to react? Through violence. When I think of those kids I'm always reminded of my friend from high school who had cerebral palsy and was confined to a wheelchair. She never thought of herself as a cripple. She simply accepted her body as the karma she'd been dealt. Instead of using it as an excuse for exuding a negativity that would have drawn more negativity to her, she went on to college and earned a degree in social work, turning her disability into an opportunity to help others.

So what was the difference between my friend and the kids at Columbine? There are actually two issues at work here. The first is that these kids could have chosen to get off the wheel of karma and react differently to those who were tormenting them. And the second is that all the negative energy they were putting out was actually drawing more negative energy to them. If you saw the movie *Ghostbusters*, you may remember that the evil slime or "ectoplasm" actually grew and reacted when people put out negativity. In other words, negative energy is drawn to and increases other negative energy.

On the other hand—because there always is another hand—the terrible events of that day created a new awareness on a global level not only of the need to create greater safety in our schools but also of the need to be more aware of how we treat those who are different from ourselves.

You are not a gerbil, so you don't need to keep
running around on the wheel of karma,
getting nowhere fast.

For every action, there is a reaction, and when the action affects large groups of people, there will be many different reactions. My personal reaction to the gift I've been given is that I ought to give a gift in return. One way that I do this is by donating to charity a portion of the proceeds from all my public appearances—in my case it's specifically breast cancer. But however we give back, it's an opportunity to open and enrich the soul.

In a sense, I believe that we create these man-made disasters because, as souls, we are meant to be tested. And those who create them are those who have elected not to "get off the wheel of karma" and grow. Instead they keep coming back and doing the same terrible things over and over again. In other words, some souls simply refuse to be rehabilitated. These are the souls who continue to bring evil into the world. People are constantly asking why, if there is a God or a higher power, evil, starvation, violence, and other "bad things" exist. My answer to that is—as I've been saying from the beginning—we have free will, we create our own karma, and we're the ones who bring evil as well as good into the world and into our lives.

While many people are perfectly comfortable accepting the concept of heaven, they are unwilling to accept the fact that there is evil in the world.

That's not to say, however, that people can't change. They can and do. People can be rehabilitated in prison, drug addicts can kick their habit, and alcoholics can recover. One thing that's always been interesting to me is that very often, once their rehabilitation takes place, these people are likely to pass over. I believe that's because once they've done their work and learned the lesson they were here to learn, it's time for them to move on.

The terrorist attacks of September 11, 2001, which, for most people, have become defining acts of man's inhumanity to man, were created by people who had been influenced by their negative belief in a perverted version of Islam. The terrorists were determined to create shock and awe, and they succeeded. But their acts also caused many of us to change the way we think about life and death. They changed thousands of lives on a personal level—not only the lives of those who died or lost loved ones but also the lives of thousands and thousands of others who determined to do things differently from that point on. And again, those changes could be for better or worse.

> When bad things happen on a global scale, there's a shift in the global consciousness.

For most people, the events of that day were a wake-up call to be kinder to one another, to be more loving, and to cherish life; for some, however, the message was just the opposite—life is short, life is unfair, so take advantage when and where you can and don't worry about anyone else. Some people just think that if they continue to look out for themselves they're somehow protecting themselves from being hurt. But, of course, just the opposite is true.

> Always looking out for number one is a sure
> way to prevent your soul from growing and
> evolving.

How many times can I say it? It's always up to us to decide whether we're going to use a particular circumstance to evolve on a soul level or whether we're going to be stubborn and refuse to acknowledge what's staring us right in the face.

And as with tragedies of nature, the most horrendous man-made disaster will bring out the greatness in some of us. Think, for example, of Mayor Rudy Giuliani. Before 9/11 he was struggling as a mayor, going through a very public divorce, and battling prostate cancer. After 9/11 he emerged as an iconic hero throughout the world. Think of Winston Churchill who, before World War II, had been effectively banished from office and put out to pasture only to return and become the inspirational leader who saw Great Britain through her darkest and also her brightest hour.

But it wasn't just these specific individuals who rose to the occasion. In the case of 9/11, the people of New York, and of the entire country, underwent a shift in consciousness, as did the British during the war. Throughout history, in fact—from the fall of the Roman Empire to the Inquisition, the Crusades, the Holocaust, the attack on Pearl Harbor, and the bombing of Hiroshima, to the attacks on the World Trade Center and the Pentagon—there have been pivotal moments at which the consciousness of the world was changed.

IT'S ALWAYS PART OF THE JOURNEY

When bad things happen, whether imposed by nature or created by man, some people begin to live with more fear because they simply don't understand that, in the journey of the soul, you sometimes have to go through these kinds of tragedies. They may turn to religion for an explanation or try to justify in some way what's taken place, but there really is no justification for these kinds of events. They are simply part of the soul's journey, and—both individually and collectively—we have to experience these challenges.

In the wake of such horrific disasters, there are always those who are able to pick themselves up and move on. I call these people spiritual nomads because they have the capacity to start over, no matter what the situation. And there are also those who are derailed, literally stopped in their tracks. These are the ones who allow their fears to prevent them from learning and growing.

What I take from this is that we as a people need to use our fear as an opportunity for growth, just as we do on a personal level. And, more often than not, many people do grow as souls. Even though they are fearful, they renew their faith in humanity, and, interestingly, in the wake of such tragedies the birthrate tends to go up. When large numbers of souls go out, large numbers also come in. Yet another sign of renewal.

Use adversity as a way to renew your faith
in humanity.

TURBULENCE IN THE WORLD OF SPIRIT

One thing I've noticed is that whenever a disaster is about to occur on a global scale, the spirit world reacts. There are storms and turbulence on the other side. I know this because I invariably get an uneasy feeling even though I don't know what's causing it. I may even think it's coming from something on a personal level and realize only after the fact what was really causing my unease.

I know people are going to think that since I'm "so psychic" I ought to know not just that "something" is going to happen but exactly what it is. All I can say is that when something's happening on such a global scale, the energy is so intense that it's simply impossible to pinpoint exactly where it's coming from. And, yes, that does make me crazy, but I've learned to accept and deal with it.

I call it a ripple in the universe, and I believe it's because the spirits are aware of the many new souls who will soon be entering the spirit realm. What we all need to understand is that even though so much death and destruction may seem senseless to us, for all those who die, it is part of their path. Despite the fact that we may not be able to see the reason, all those who go out in these mass exoduses have picked that time to go.

SOUL PRINTS

* ✽ Global tragedy is an opportunity for large groups of people to learn and to grow.
* ✽ When Nature destroys, it also creates opportunities for rebirth.
* ✽ Man-made evil is created by souls who refuse to learn and be rehabilitated.
* ✽ After every monumental tragedy, either natural or created by man, there will be unlikely heroes who rise to the occasion.
* ✽ Creating good karma always means giving back for whatever gifts have come our way.
* ✽ Experiencing these kinds of challenges is part of our soul path.
* ✽ Although it's difficult to accept, all those who die as a result of such far-reaching disasters have chosen their way to go out.

9

Clear the Clutter and Tap in to Your Own Soul Potential

I've been saying all along that each one of us comes into the world with a kind of road map our soul is intended to follow. And I have to repeat that even though we may not achieve greatness in the sense that we produce a world-changing invention, write a great symphony, or become a world-class athlete, we all, in our own small way, can make a difference in this world while we're here.

> "I have come to realize that in every person there is something fine and pure and noble, along with a desire for self-fulfillment."
> —*Jimmy Carter*

Most of us also come in with a lot of useless baggage we're still hauling around from one or more previous lives, and the longer we continue to weigh ourselves down by hanging on to to all the stuff we should have discarded, the harder it will be for us to rise to a higher level of soul consciousness. I'm sure that at some point in your life you've cleaned out a room or a closet that was full of junk you hadn't even looked at in years. When you got done, you probably felt liberated from all that old, dusty stuff you may not even have known you still had. And then what happened? Suddenly you had a lot of room for new, better, more useful stuff. Well, it works the same way with your soul.

CLEARING THE SOUL CLUTTER

If you keep hanging on to emotions, habits, beliefs, jobs, people—you name it—that haven't been working for you, your life will continue to be cluttered with useless garbage and you won't be able to make room for anything that's newer and better. So why do you do it? Probably for the same reasons you kept all that old stuff in the closet—you may be so used to having it around that you don't even think about it anymore, you may be afraid to let it go because you're not sure you'll be able to replace it, or you may fear that if you do replace it, the new thing you bring in may not be any better than the old one you threw away. When it comes to your soul potential, however, just getting rid of whatever it is that's been weighing you down may, in and of itself, be enough to let you rise to a new level of peace and fulfillment. Clearing the clutter may be all you need to give you an expanded vision of what lies ahead.

With a clear mind you can see forever.

If you're going to clear the clutter, the first thing you need to do is open the closet door and take a good look at what's in there. Are you harboring fears that prevent you from trying something new? Are you hanging on to a boring, unfulfilling job because you're afraid you'll never get another one? Are there people in your life who always seem to make you feel bad but you don't know how to cut them loose? If so, you really need to ask yourself, "What have I got to lose? I'm not happy, I don't feel fulfilled, I'm in a rut, so why not try something different?"

Then, before you decide to slam the door again and leave things as they were, ask yourself another question. "If I didn't have all this negative stuff in my life, what would I be able to bring into it that I really want? What am I missing that I want to bring into my life?" I think you know. I think that on the psychic level we all know when our soul purpose is not being fulfilled. It's just that some of us have more junk than others obscuring our clarity of vision. And some of us are more stubborn than others about hanging on to what we know even if we know it isn't working anymore. As I've said, I was one of the stubborn ones who spent years trying to deny and run away from my true calling.

That's probably also what makes me particularly adept at knowing when other people are doing the same thing, and why sometimes I find it so annoying. With some people, no matter how many times I tell them *this is what you're supposed to be doing,* they just don't get it—or maybe they don't *want* to get it. Maybe like old Isaac Newton they need an apple to fall on their head and knock some sense into them.

Such was the case for Karen, who was terribly afraid of repeating the pattern of her parents' unhappy marriage but who, despite my warnings, did, in fact, marry a man who turned out to be exactly like her father. Like her father, Karen's husband had been charming at first but had gradually become more and more abusive. Before they were married I had tried to make her aware of the patterns she was repeating. Her husband-to-be was already showing himself to be arrogant, demanding, and controlling, and I had been telling her that she was about to marry her father, but she simply wouldn't, or couldn't, hear what I was saying.

Happily, with counseling, Karen and her husband were able to change the pattern of their relationship and save their marriage, but not until she had gone through a tremendous amount of heartache and had gotten to the brink of losing her identity and self-esteem just as her mother had.

BREAKING THE PATTERN

If you see yourself repeating destructive or self-defeating patterns in your life, it's a pretty good bet that you did the same thing in a previous life. In fact, if you're doing something that's making you unhappy and you still can't stop doing it, you can pretty much use that as a clue to what you're supposed to be learning and haven't. Just being aware of that is your first step toward breaking the pattern.

When I asked Dr. Brian Weiss, the well-known psychiatrist, author, and authority on past-life regression, for his thoughts on the subject, this is what he had to say.

DR. BRIAN WEISS—IN HIS OWN WORDS

"I've done past-life regressions now with more than four thousand patients over the course of twenty-five years, and what I find is that patterns keep repeating themselves until they're understood and resolved. One of our purposes in being born, and along the spiritual journey, is to learn these lessons—about love, patience, compassion, understanding, nonviolence—and what happens is that we get more than one chance to get it right. That's my understanding of past lives and reincarnation. And so, if there is a pattern there—for example, of violence—you have to learn that it is not the spiritual action to harm other beings. If you're a violent person, and you haven't stopped being a violent person, you're somehow going to be visited by the negative effects of violence in your lifetime. Violence inflicted on you or on people you care about—something that will show you that violence is not the way. And until you stop and understand that, it will keep happening.

"I see the same thing in relationships. Until you treat others with compassion and dignity and respect and understanding, your relationships will not be completely fulfilling. Or there might be a pattern of substance abuse. You might have found in a past life that that was a shortcut or a way of facing a situation, and, if so, there will be a tendency for you to do the same thing in this life when you're faced with that difficult situation, which is being brought back to you so that you can learn from it. The obstacles that we face in life are often opportunities for learning and growth.

"One pattern that does keep repeating and that I've written a lot about is suicide—not from severe mental illness or intractable pain, but something like a business failure or shame. People who have committed suicide successfully in a past life will often in a future life be confronted with some of the same situations, because they have to learn that the body is very important and they're being given the opportunity to deal with the situation differently than they did in the past.

"It may be a cliché, but it appears that there really are no coincidences. These situations for learning and growth are given to us as steps for us to use along the way. By doing a past-life regression, you immediately grasp the whole nature of the pattern, and when you have that understanding, you can change things. I see this on all levels. For instance, someone might have a water phobia because he drowned in a past life. Once he sees that it's the past, that it already happened, it isn't going to happen in the future; he knows where the phobia is coming from and it usually disappears.

"This is really very similar to traditional therapy. The only difference is that instead of stopping at infancy it takes it one step further. It's the same concept—by uncovering the forgotten memory, healing takes place. It's a more profound kind of healing than, for example, behavior modification, because it gets to the source. By going to the source and understanding it, that's how you can truly eliminate it.

"Past-life regression is helpful in many different ways. One is that you lose your fear of death and dying. You've died many times, you still existed, you came back here, and your loved ones are in the same process. The consciousness or the soul or the spirit or whatever you want to call it never really dies. So when you see that and experience it, you see yourself, and now you're back again, that's very liberating.

"People don't believe in it, and that's fine. I was totally skeptical until I had these experiences. But all they have to do is try it. It's not so complicated. I use hypnosis—which is very misunderstood because of the way it's been represented in the movies and on television. It's really just a state of deep relaxation and focused concentration. You're not asleep, no one takes over anyone's body, you don't do anything you don't want to do. It's like being engrossed in a movie or a good book so that you don't pay attention to outside stimuli and distractions—that's hypnosis, that's all it is. I use it because in that very relaxed and concentrated state the memory is enhanced and people can remember more—so it's a shortcut into the past."

———

Do you keep getting into the same kinds of dead-end, disappointing relationships? Do you continuously turn down opportunities that come knocking at your door? Do you repeat destructive patterns of behavior? Believe me, if that's the case, you've done it before in another life and you need to get past whatever it is that's blocking you from doing something different. For people who are open and willing to listen, seeing someone like me can really help. Maybe just because I've been doing it for so long (or maybe because it's built into my own soul path) I usually know instinctively what to say to people, and how to say it, to give them the information they need without hurting them or causing them to shut down.

When we build up walls to protect ourselves, we're really creating our own prison. By dismantling our defenses, we free ourselves to grow and soar.

Sometimes, however, even I realize that the protective walls my client has built up are too well fortified for me to break down. If that's the case, as I've said, I strongly suggest that the person see a traditional therapist to help him or her work through whatever it is that's preventing him or her from really hearing what I have to say.

One young woman had been abandoned by her father as a child and was now becoming involved with one guy after another who was unable to commit. As a result, she was constantly being abandoned. I kept telling her, over and over, that she was putting out negative energy that was attracting only "bad boys" and continuing to re-create the relationship she'd had with her father. But no matter how many times we discussed it, she was simply unable to change. Finally, after about a year and a half of this, I told her that she really needed to see a therapist who could help her to resolve whatever issues she still had with her father that were being self-destructively repeated in her current relationships.

Saddest of all is when I see someone throwing his or her life away because of something left unresolved in his or her past. One particularly heart-wrenching incidence of this involved a client who believed that she was responsible for the death of her sister when they were small children and was now living in deathly fear that she would somehow harm her own child. During my reading, the sister came through and showed me the truth—that it had really been a tragic accident.

It seemed that the two little girls had been running in the backyard when my client's sister ran into the empty clothesline and the lollipop she had in her mouth lodged in her throat and choked her. Because her parents were unable to deal with their own guilt and resolve their own feelings about the accident, they had allowed my client to carry her own unwarranted feelings of guilt without ever explaining what had really happened.

Even after that initial reading, however, she was unable to let go of her guilt. No matter how hard I tried to convince her over the course of the next year, she was unable to accept what I was saying. She was having panic attacks and her husband was on the verge of leaving her when I finally convinced her to allow herself to be hypnotized in order to bring up and actually remember what had happened. Only then was she able to unblock her mind and accept the truth, which allowed her to release her guilt as well as her unfounded fears.

BE OPEN, ASK, AND YOU WILL RECEIVE

If you're willing to part with your personal garbage and open yourself up to filling your life with something that's more rewarding, something that will make you feel more successful as a human being, you *can*, I promise you, bring it into your life.

Remember that on a soul level you are energy, and all energy can be either positive or negative. Simply by releasing the old, negative energy that's been pulling you in the wrong direction, you can start to put forth a new, positive energy that will draw what you want and need into your life like a magnet.

When you exude positive energy,
positive things will come your way.

Since ancient times, people have been using various means of focusing their minds so that they are better able to "see" their true path. Perhaps the oldest of these tools is the *I Ching*, one of the fundamental books of Confucianism that dates back almost three thousand years. To use the *I Ching* as a means of tapping in to psychic energy, one casts a group of coins in a particular pattern and then consults the book to determine what the pattern means. Similar to the *I Ching*, and almost as ancient, is the runic alphabet discovered in what is now Eastern Europe more than fifteen hundred years ago. Each rune or symbol is inscribed on a stone and the stones are thrown to form various patterns that are then studied to determine their meaning. Either one of these methods provides a means for us to analyze the path we are on and, if we determine that it is not the road to fulfillment, figure out how to change paths and, thus, open our soul to a more positive flow of energy.

Tarot cards, which originated in northern Italy more than five hundred years ago as a tool for spiritual introspection, and even the Ouija board, which was actually brought to America as a parlor game, are also among the many devices we can use to call upon and concentrate our psychic or soul energy.

The key word here is "energy," whether it's coming from souls who have passed on or those still living on this plane. Auras, which I discussed in my previous book, are created by the energy of the living, and their color is affected by the kind of energy that person is giving off. By seeing a person's aura, I am able to determine, for example, whether he or she is in good mental and/or physical health, whether he or she is artistic, spiritually enlightened, honest, and so on. And I can see, when I meet the same person on more than one occasion, whether his or her energy has changed, because if it has, his or her aura will also have changed.

Psychometry is another way to tap in to the energy of the living (as well as the dead). It is the art of gaining information about an object or anything related to that object by holding it in your hand. If we touch something, some of our energy is transferred to that object and remains there, so making contact with the object connects us to the energy of the person with whom it is associated.

The same is true of a photograph. The energy of a living person is transferred to the photograph, which means that simply by looking at the photo I am able to gather information about the person whose image it is.

MEDITATION—A POWERFUL PSYCHIC TOOL

One of the best ways I know to tap into your own living energy is through meditation, something I also discussed in my previous book. Some people seem to be afraid to meditate (possibly for the same reason some people are afraid of hypnosis—they somehow believe it will cause them to relinquish control). Others use the excuse that they just don't have the time. To the former I say, like everything in life, what you fear may be your best opportunity for learning. To the latter I say, just take two or three minutes a day and start. Once you do that, you'll begin to open yourself up to your higher, psychic self. Or, to put it another way, open the door between here and the afterlife. Believe me when I say that the reward will be far greater than whatever time and energy you put into it.

I also offer a word of caution. There are negative spirits in the world as well as positive ones. You want to attract the good, not the bad, so I always suggest that you begin your meditation with a prayer. It doesn't matter what kind of prayer; that's up to you, and it may depend on your personal religious belief.

INVITE YOUR SPIRIT GUIDE INTO YOUR LIFE

Spirit guides often come to us in the form of someone we've met in a previous life. They are different from our loved ones in spirit, who come to us out of the love we've shared in this life.

We all have spirit guides. In fact, I have found that we may have different spirit guides at different stages in our life. It all depends on what your mission is and what point you've arrived at on your soul path. As you pray and learn to meditate, you will open your mind and make a space for your spirit guide to come through. Different people in different cultures have had a variety of ways to do this. Native Americans, for example, went into a special place called a sweat lodge and prayed to the Great Spirit to put them on the right path. Today, the closest most of us get to a sweat lodge is the sauna at the gym, but we can still put ourselves in the proper frame of mind for communicating with the world of spirit.

When you ask for guidance, those in spirit will lead you in the right direction.

You can ask for a sign from your spirit guide. Do this before you go to sleep—which is also a way, as I've said, to invite a dream visit from a loved one in spirit—or do what I do and spend a few minutes at the start of your day asking for what you need to bring into your life.

I call these prayerful requests my daily thoughts. I ask for what I need, and then I say that I need a sign, and I need it to be very specific and unique. In other words, I need to be able to recognize it when I see it. As an example of how unique a sign can be—and how we can still fail to recognize it when we see it—I had client who had always been obsessed with Native Americans. She didn't know why, but she had always found Native Americans and their history fascinating. Wherever this woman went, a feather would turn up, even in the most unlikely locations—on the beach, in her own back-yard, in the parking lot of the local mall. She noticed them, of course, but it never occurred to her that they had any special significance—until I sat with her and did a reading during which her spirit guide came through. I told her, "Your guide is showing me a feather. He says he's been sending you a feather. Why are you not paying attention? He's getting very frustrated with you." And then I described the feather he was showing me. It was large and looked almost like an eagle feather, but, in fact, it was a seagull feather that her spirit guide—who actually let me know that his name was One Feather—was showing me. It's possible, I believe, that this woman had been a Native American in a past life, and that's why she was so fascinated with them, as well as why her spirit guide turned out to be a Native American.

As I've said, we all have spirit guides and all we need to do is ask them to help us. Talk to them; say a prayer. The power of prayer—however you pray—is unique in my experience. We know that there's evil in the world, or, more often, misguided human beings, and there are also misguided spirits, but prayer has the power to pull in what I call the good souls.

It's possible that when you begin to open up to the

world of spirit, you'll have to deal with some earthbound spirits who want to play games with you (often these are the mischievous poltergeists I talked about earlier), but you don't have to acknowledge them or allow them to get to you. You can simply tell them they're not welcome and ask them politely to go away, and in most instances they'll leave you alone.

At the other end of the spectrum from those troublemaking, earthbound spirits are guardian angels, highly evolved souls who may or may not have been directly related to us in life but who watch over us from the other side. My client Julie, for instance, believes that she was saved from drowning in a rip current through divine intervention. She said that she knew "something" had lifted her up and moved her out of the deadly current—and it wasn't Charlie the Tuna!

"The delight of the wisdom of the angels is
to communicate to others what they know."
—*Emanuel Swedenborg*

In earlier chapters I talked about the ways loved ones in spirit have intervened to protect or guide their loved ones in situations where, according to all that we know on a logical level, they should have died. In those instances, their loved ones were acting as guardian angels. In one situation, a female police officer who was the third of four children had a brother who died very young of an incurable lung disorder. Her brother in spirit then became attached to her and stuck around to act as her spirit guide and guardian angel, and she says that now, whenever her job takes her into a dangerous situation, she can feel her brother's presence watching over her.

OPEN THE DOOR—IT WILL MAKE YOUR LIFE RICHER

The one thought I want to leave you with here is that you have nothing to fear from the world of spirit. On the contrary, allowing yourself to tap into your own spirituality will broaden and enrich your life experience—as it has mine—in ways you may never have imagined.

Many of us who are of a certain age remember the old television game show on which the host Monty Hall asked contestants in the audience to choose "door number one, door number two, or door number three." I'm telling you that there is another door—call it door number four if you want. It is a door to another world, a world beyond the earthly plane, just waiting for you to open it.

SOUL PRINTS

* We all come into the world with a road map for reaching our potential, but we also carry a lot of heavy baggage that can make the journey more difficult than it needs to be.
* Stop hanging on to old emotions, beliefs, fears, jobs, people—whatever is weighing you down or preventing you from tapping in to your true soul potential.
* Negative patterns are almost always holdovers from past-life experiences.

✳ If you can discover what happened to you in a past life that's negatively affecting your present life, you will almost always be able to resolve it.

✳ Seeing a psychic or a therapist can help you to get to the root of why you're repeating negative patterns so that you will be able to move forward.

✳ Once you release your negative energy, you will be opening up pathways through which new, positive energy will flow.

✳ Meditation is a powerful tool for helping you release negative energy.

✳ Meditation will help you get in touch with your spirit guides, who can set you on the right path.

✳ Ask prayerfully for what you need to come into your life, and it will come.

Resources

ORGANIZATIONS AND WEBSITES

American Association of Electronic Voice Phenomena
www.aaevp.com
provides education and support for people interested in EVP

Dr. Brian Weiss's website
www.brianweiss.com

The Compassionate Friends
www.compassionatefriends.org
is a self-help and support group for parents who have lost
children; approximately six hundred chapters throughout
the United States

Jeffrey Wands's website
www.jeffreywands.com

National Center for Missing and Exploited Children
www.missingkids.com
offers resources for parents and guardians, advice on what
to do and how to report a missing child, and a twenty-
four–hour hotline

RESOURCES

Dr. Raymond Moody's website
www.lifeafterlife.com

BOOKS

The Afterlife Connection: A Therapist Reveals How to Communicate with Departed Loved Ones by Dr. Jane Greer. St. Martin's Press, 2003.

The Afterlife Experiments: Breakthrough Scientific Evidence of Life After Death by Gary E. Schwartz, Ph.D. Pocket Books, 2002.

Dogs That Know When Their Owners Are Coming Home: And Other Unexplained Powers of Animals by Rupert Sheldrake. Three Rivers Press, 2000.

I'm Still Here by Martha Pierce Copeland. AA-EVP Publishing, 2005.

Life After Life: The Investigation of a Phenomenon—Survival of Bodily Death by Raymond A. Moody, Jr., M.D. Harper San Francisco, 2001.

Many Lives, Many Masters: The True Story of a Prominent Psychiatrist, His Young Patient, and the Past-Life Therapy That Changed Both Their Lives by Brian L. Weiss, M.D. Fireside, 1988.

On Life After Death by Elisabeth Kübler-Ross. Celestial Arts, 1991.

The Psychic in You: Understand and Harness Your Natural Psychic Power by Jeffrey A. Wands. Atria Books, 2004.